HIGH TOR

A Play in Three Acts

By
MAXWELL ANDERSON

ANDERSON HOUSE
Washington, D.C.
1 9 3 7

NOTE

GEORGE BANTA PUBLISHING COMPANY, MENASHA, WISCONSIN

Guthrie McClintic presented Maxwell Anderson's HIGH
TOR for the first time on any stage in the Hanna Theater,
Cleveland, Ohio, Wednesday night, December 30, 1936,
with this cast:

THE INDIAN	*Harry Irvine*
VAN VAN DORN	*Burgess Meredith*
JUDITH	*Mab Maynard*
ART. J. BIGGS	*Harold Moffet*
JUDGE SKIMMERHORN	*Thomas W. Ross*
LISE	*Peggy Ashcroft*
CAPTAIN ASHER	*Byron McGrath*
PIETER	*John Philliber*
A SAILOR	*William Casamo*
DEWITT	*Charles D. Brown*
DOPE	*Leslie Gorall*
ELKUS	*Hume Cronyn*
BUDDY	*John Drew Colt*
PATSY	*Charles Forrester*
A. B. SKIMMERHORN	*John M. Kline*
BUDGE	*Jackson Halliday*

DUTCH CREW OF THE *Onrust*

The play was staged by Mr. McClintic and the settings
were designed by Jo Mielziner.

HIGH TOR

ACT ONE

ACT ONE

SCENE I

SCENE: *A section of the broad flat trap-rock summit of High Tor, from which one looks out into sky and from which one might look down a sheer quarter mile to the Tappan Zee below. A cluster of hexagonal pillared rocks masks the view to the left and a wind-tortured small hemlock wedges into the rock floor at the right. Light from the setting sun pours in from the left, and an ancient* INDIAN, *wearing an old greatcoat thrown round him like a blanket, stands in the rays from a cleft, making his prayer to the sunset.*

The Indian. I make my prayer to you, the falling fire,
   bearing in mind the whisper in my ears
   from the great spirit, talking on the wind,
   whispering that a young race, in its morning,
   should pray to the rising sun, but a race that's old
   and dying, should invoke the dying flame
   eaten and gulfed by the shark-toothed mountain-west,
   a god that dies to live. As we have died,
   my race of the red faces and old ways,
   and as we hope to rise. I give you thanks
   for light, for the coming summer that will warm
   my snake's blood, cold and crawling; for the rain
   that fed the ripe May apples in the woods
   in secret for me; for the waterfall
   where the trout climb and pause under my hand,
   taken in silence; for quiet on the hills
   where the loud races dare not walk for fear
   lest they be lost, where their blind hunters pass
   peering with caps and guns, but see no game,
   and curse as they go down, while the raccoon waits,
   the woodchuck stands erect to catch the wind,

3

the partridge steps so lightly over leaves
the listening fox hears nothing, the possum hangs
head down, looking through his hands, and takes no
                              breath,
the gray squirrel turns to stone against the rock,
watching the owl, the rabbit holds his ears
steady above the trembling of his heart
and the crow mocks down the shellbark. I am fed
and sheltered on this mountain where their hands
are helpless. But I am old as my race is old;
my eyes hunt day and night along the ground
the grave where I shall lie; my ears have heard
dead women calling upward from the earth,
mother and wife and child: "You are welcome here;
you are no longer welcome where you walk,
but here you are most welcome." I shall go,
and lie and sleep, and I shall give you thanks,
O God that dies, that my last night is dark
and long, for I am tired, but yet I ask
one summer more, that I may be warm again,
and watch the nestlings grown upon the crag,
and hear the wild geese honking south by night,
if this may be, but if it may not be
then is my prayer, that when I lie to sleep
I may lie long, sleep soundly, hear no step,
hear only through the earth your step in spring,
O God of the dying fire!

[VAN DORN *and* JUDITH *come in from the right.*]

Van Dorn. Evening, John.

The Indian. Evening.

Van Dorn. Had any luck so far?

The Indian. Yes. Plenty of luck.

Van Dorn. Found it?

The Indian. Yes.

Van Dorn. O.K., John, let me know.
Let me know in time.

The Indian. I will. Good night.

Van Dorn. Good night.

[*The* INDIAN *slips away through the rocks to the left.*]

Judith. Who is it, Van?

Van. Just an Indian.

Judith. Are there Indians?
I didn't know there were any Indians left.

Van. Well, there's one. There's not much left of him,
and he's the last around here.

Judith. He's hunting something?
You asked him if he'd found it.

Van. Um—yes, you see,
he's looking for a place to make his grave,
and he's kind of captious about it—folks get that way
along toward the end, wanting their bones done up
in some particular fashion. Maybe because
that's all you've got to leave about that time
and you want it the way you want it.

Judith. Did he tell you this?

Van. We've got an understanding. When he feels it
coming over him he's going to die

he'll let me know, and I'll go dig him in
so the crows and foxes can't get at him. See,
he's all alone in the world. We fixed this up
a couple of years ago.

Judith. But you couldn't Van,
without a permit. A burial permit.

Van. Oh,
I guess you could. This getting old and dying
and crawling into the ground, that was invented
back before medical examiners
and taxes and all that. The old boy's clean.
He'll go right back to dirt.

Judith. But, Van, you can't!
People can't die that way!

Van. I guess they can.
What the hell good's being wrapped in cellophane?
You don't keep anyway.

Judith. You're impossible
to live with! Why do you say such things? If I
should die—you'd get a pine box!—

Van. If you should die
the old boy that drives the sun around up there,
he'd unhitch, and put the cattle out
to grass, and give it up. He'd plumb lose interest
if you should die. Maybe I would myself,
I don't say. Maybe I would.—Fetch out that supper.
We want to see what we eat.

Judith.
   [*Opening a lunch box*]

It's dinner, Van,
not supper.

Van. That's what I said. Fetch out that dinner.
When it gets a little darker what's black's pepper
and what's green's parsley; still you can't be sure.
It might be ants.

Judith. Just the same we'll quarrel.
We'll always quarrel.

Van. Oh, no. We've both got sense.
What's the sense fighting?
  [*He looks at a paper that was round the lunch.*]

Judith. And you shouldn't read at table.

Van. I never do. The Nanuet bank's been robbed.
My God, there's not enough money in Nanuet
to buy their gas for a get-away. One night
pap and me sat in on a poker game
in Nanuet and took twenty-seven dollars
out of town. Next day they couldn't do business.
The place was clean.

Judith. There were troopers at the train
tonight, and sirens going through Haverstraw,
but the robbers got away.

Van. They took twenty-five thousand.
How'd twenty-five thousand get to Nanuet?
It's against nature.

Judith. It didn't stay there long.

Van. No—I understand that.
But just to have it there in passing, just

to look at, just to fool the customers,
how do they do it?

Judith. Maybe it wasn't real.

Van. Federal money, that's it. Some of the stuff
Jim Farley prints in Washington with the stamps
to pay you for voting straight. Only now you see it
and now you don't.

Judith. They say it buys as much
as if you earned it.

Van. Bad for the stomach, though,
to live on humble pie.

Judith. I'd rather work.

Van. Well, as I said, don't work if you don't feel like it.
Any time you want to move up in the hills
and sleep with me, it's a bargain.

Judith. Van!

Van. Why not?
We'll get married if that's what you mean.

Judith. You haven't any job. And you make it sound
like animals.

Van. I'm fond of animals.

Judith. You shoot them all the time.

Van. Well, I get hungry.
Any man's liable to get hungry.

Judith. Van,
I want to talk to you seriously.

Van. Can't be done.
   Listen, things get serious enough
   without setting out to do it.

Judith. Van, this spring
   you had three weeks' work, laying dry wall.
   You could have had more, but you didn't take it.
   You're an expert mason—

Van. I'm good at everything.

Judith. But you work three weeks in the year—

Van. That's all I need—

Judith. And all the rest of the year you hunt or fish
   or sleep, or God knows what—

Van. Ain't it the truth?

Judith. Last fall I came looking for you once, and you
   were gone—gone to Port Jervis hunting—deer,
   you said on the postcard—

Van. Sure, I was hunting deer—
   didn't I bring you half a venison?

Judith. But not a word to me till I got the postcard
   ten days later—

Van. Didn't have a minute—

Judith. Then last winter there's a note nailed to a tree
   and you're in Virginia, down in the Dismal Swamp
   tracking bear. Now, for God's sake, Van,
   it's no way to live.

Van. Jeez, it's a lot of fun.

Judith. Maybe for you.

Van. You want me to take that job.

Judith. Why don't you, Van?

Van. Porter in a hotel, lugging up satchels,
opening windows, maybe you get a dime.
I'd choke to death.

Judith. I'd see you every day.

Van. Yeah, I could see you on the mezzanine,
taking dictation from the drummer boys,
all about how they can't get home. You can stand it,
a woman stands that stuff, but if you're a man
I say it chokes you.

Judith. We can't live in your cabin
and have no money, like the Jackson Whites
over at Suffern.

Van. Hell, you don't need money.
Pap worked that out. All you need's a place to sleep
and something to eat. I've never seen the time
I couldn't find a meal on the mountain here,
rainbow trout, jugged hare, something in season
right around the zodiac.

Judith. You didn't like
the Chevrolet factory, either?

Van.

   [*Walking toward the cliff edge*]

Look at it, Judy.
That's the Chevrolet factory, four miles down,
and straight across, that's Sing Sing. Right from here

you can't tell one from another; get inside,
and what's the difference? You're in there, and you
                                            work,
and they've got you. If you're in the factory
you buy a car, and then you put in your time
to pay for the goddam thing. If you get in a hurry
and steal a car, they put you in Sing Sing first,
and then you work out your time. They graduate
from one to the other, back and forth, those guys,
paying for cars both ways. But I was smart.
I parked at a polis station and rung the bell
and took to the woods. Not for your Uncle Dudley.
They plugged the dice.

Judith. But one has to have a car.

Van. Honest to God now, Judy, what's the hurry?
Where in hell are we going?

Judith. If a man works hard,
and has ability, as you have, Van,
he takes a place among them, saves his money,
works right out of the ruck and gets above
where he's safe and secure.

Van. I wouldn't bet on it much.

Judith. But it's true.

Van. All right, suppose it's true. Suppose
a man saves money all his life, and works
like hell about forty years, till he can say:
good-bye, I'm going, I'm on easy street
from now on. What's he do?

Judith. Takes a vacation.

Van. Goes fishing, maybe? I'm on vacation now.
  Why should I work forty years to earn
  time off when I've got it?

Judith. It's not always easy,
  you know it's not. There was that time last winter
  when I helped you out.

Van. Why, sure, you helped me out.
  Why wouldn't you? But if you didn't help me
  I'd get along.

Judith. Yes, you would. I know you would.
  But you don't even seem to want money. You won't
                    take it
  when they bring it to you.

Van. When did they bring me any?

Judith. And what if there was a child?

Van. Why he'd be fine—
  the less they have the better they like it.—Oh,
  you mean the trap-rock company, wanting to buy
  High Tor? They offered seven hundred dollars—
  and they offered pap ten thousand before he died,
  and he wouldn't sell.

Judith. He wouldn't?

Van. They want to chew
  the back right off this mountain, the way they did
  across the clove there. Leave the old palisades
  sticking up here like billboards, nothing left
  but a false front facing the river. Not for pap,
  and not for me. I like this place.

Judith. But, Van Van Dorn!
Ten thousand dollars!

Van. Well, it's Federal money.
Damn stuff evaporates. Put it in a sock
along with moth balls, and come back next year,
and there's nothing left but the smell. Look, Judy, it's
a quarter mile straight down to the Tappan Zee
from here.—You can see fifteen miles of river
north and south. I grew up looking at it.
Hudson came up that river just about
three hundred years ago, and lost a ship
here in the Zee. They say the crew climbed up
this Tor to keep a lookout for the fleet
that never came. Maybe the Indians got them.
Anyway on dark nights before a storm,
they say you sometimes see them.

Judith. Have you seen them?

Van. The Dutchmen? Maybe I have. You can't be sure.
It's pretty wild around here when it storms.
That's when I like it best. But look at it now.
There was a Jaeger here from Switzerland
last year. He took one squint at this and said
they could keep their Alps, for all him. Look at the
                                    willows
along the far breakwater.

Judith. It's beautiful.

Van. Every night I come back here like the Indian
to get a fill of it. Seven hundred dollars
and tear it down? Hell, no.
   [BIGGS *and* SKIMMERHORN *come in from the right, a bit be·*

draggled, and wiping their brows. Skimmerhorn *carries a brief-case. It is growing darker.*]

Biggs. Hey listen, Mac, any houses round here?

Van. Guess you're off the beat, buddy; never heard of any houses on the mountain.

Skimmerhorn. Come on, Art; we're doing well if we're down at the road before dark.

Biggs. Look, Mac, maybe you can help us out. You familiar with this region, at all?

Van. I've been around here some.

Biggs. Well, we're all afternoon hunting a cabin that's somewhere along the ridge. Ever hear of it?

Van. Anybody live in it?

Biggs. Fellow named Van Dorn.

Van. Oh, yes, sure.

Biggs. You know where it is?

Van. Sure. You climb down the face of the cliff here and keep left along the ledge about a hundred yards, then you turn sharp left through a cleft up the ridge. Follow the trail about half a mile and there you are.

Skimmerhorn. Down the face of the cliff?

Van. Down through the rocks there, then turn left—

Skimmerhorn. A monkey couldn't go down there, hanging on with four hands and a tail!

Van. Well, you can always walk along back toward Little Tor, and cut down from there through the gulch.

There's a slough at the bottom of the ravine, but if you get through that you can see the cabin up on the side-hill. About four miles that way.

Skimmerhorn. Yeah, we'll set right out. I always did want to get lost up here and spend a night in the hills.

Van. Oh, you'll get lost, all right.

Biggs. Any snakes?

Van. No, you might see a copperhead, or a timber rattler.

Skimmerhorn. Coming back down?

Biggs. Yeah, we'd better go down. Thanks.

Van. Don't mention it.
    [BIGGS *and* SKIMMERHORN *go out to the right.*]

Judith. But they were looking for you?

Van. Yeah.

Judith. Why didn't you tell them?

Van. What?

Judith. Who you were!

Van. They didn't ask about that.

Judith. But out of common courtesy!

Van. Well, you see, I know who they are.

Judith. Who are they?

Van. Art J. Biggs, Junior, and Skimmerhorn, Judge Skimmerhorn.

Judith. But why not talk to them?

Van. Oh, we communicate by mail. I've got
a dozen letters stacked up from the firm:
Skimmerhorn, Skimmerhorn, Biggs and Skimmerhorn,
and maybe two or three Skimmerhorns I left out
printed across the top. They're realtors,
whatever that is, and they own the trap-rock company,
and one of the Skimmerhorns, he's probate judge,
and goes around condemning property
when they want to make a rake-off. Take a letter:
Dear Skimmerhorn—

Judith. But they're the trap-rock men!

Van. That's what I said.

Judith. I'll call them!

Van. Oh, no; oh, no!
I've got nothing to say to those two buzzards
except I hope they break their fat-back necks
on their own trap-rock.

Judith. You take a lot for granted.

Van. Do I?

Judith. You think, because I said I loved you once,
that's the end; I'm finished.

Van. Oh, far from it.

Judith. Oh, yes—you think because a girl's been kissed
she stays kissed, and after that the man
does her thinking for her.

Van. Hell, it's all I can do
to handle my own thinking.

Judith. If we're married
I'll have to live the way you want to live.
You prefer being a pauper!

Van. Get it straight!
I don't take money nor orders, and I live
as I damn well please.

Judith. But we'd live like paupers!
And you could have a fortune!

Van. Seven hundred dollars?

Judith. You could get more!

Van. I don't mean to sell at all.

Judith. You see; it's your place, and your thinking! You
decide,
but I'd have to stand it with you!

Van. What do you want?

Judith. Something to start on; and now, you see, we could
have it,
only you won't!

Van. I can't, Judy, that's the truth.
I just can't.

Judith. They'll get it anyway.
They've worked right up to where your land begins,
and they won't stop for you. They'll just condemn it
and take it.

Van. They'll be in trouble.

Judith. You can't make trouble
for companies. They have a dozen lawyers

and ride right over you. I've worked for them.
It's never any use.

Van. Well, I won't sell.

Judith. We'll call it off then.

Van. What?

Judith. Between you and me.

Van. Only you don't mean it.

Judith. I know I do, though.
    You haven't thought about it, and so you think
    I couldn't do it. But it's better now
    than later.

Van. You don't know what it means to me
    if you can say it.

Judith. It means as much to me,
    but I look ahead a little.

Van. What do you see?

Judith. Two people growing old
    and having children, running wild in the woods
    with nothing.

Van. There's no better place to run.
    But I've been counting on you. More than you know.
    More than—Judy, this is the kind of night
    we've been in love most.

Judith. Yes, we could be in love,
    but that's not everything.

Van. Well, just about.
    What else do we get?

Judith. I think I'd better go.
   It's getting dark.

Van. You could find your way by the beacon.

Judith. I'd better go.
   [BIGGS *and* SKIMMERHORN *come back from the right.*]

Biggs. Listen, Mac, would you do something for us?

Van. I don't know.

Biggs. Could you take a paper round to Van Dorn and
   leave it with him?

Van. A summons?

Biggs. A sort of notice.

Van. Yeah, a notice to appear. No, I couldn't.

Biggs. It's worth a dollar to me.

Van. I'd be cheating you.

Skimmerhorn. Make it two dollars.

Van. You'd be throwing away money.

Skimmerhorn. Never mind that part of it. Will you do it?

Van. You'll take a running jump over the edge of the
   cliff and think things over on the way down before I
   serve any papers for you.

Biggs. What's the matter with us?

Van. Might be hoof and mouth disease, for all I know.
   You certainly brought an awful stench up here with
   you.

Skimmerhorn. Not much on manners, these natives.

Van. My rule in life is keep away from skunks.

Biggs. You'll get the tar kicked out of you one of these days.

Van. Make it today.

Judith. If you gentlemen care to know, this is Mr. Van Dorn.

Biggs. Say, are you Van Dorn?

Van. Sure I am.

Biggs.

> [*Extending a hand*]

Oh, in that case, forget it—you're the fellow we want to see!—Boy, we apologize—

> [*He uncovers*]

and to the lady, too! Listen, I don't know what to say but you've got us all wrong. We want to buy this place!

Van. You like the view, I suppose?

Biggs. Certainly is a view.

Van. You wouldn't spoil it, of course? You wouldn't move in with a million dollars worth of machinery and cut the guts out of the mountain, would you?

Skimmerhorn. We always leave the front—the part you see from the river.

Van. But you take down all the law allows.

Skimmerhorn. Well, we're in business.

Van. Not with me.

Judith. Do you mind if I ask how much you're offering?

Biggs. We said seven hundred, but I'll make it a thousand right here and now.

Skimmerhorn. As a matter of fact, we'll make it two thousand.

Biggs. Yeah, all right. Two thousand for the hundred and seven acres.

Judith. But you offered Mr. Van Dorn's father ten thousand before he died.

Skimmerhorn. His father had a clear title, right down from the original Dutch patroon to the original Van Dorn. But unfortunately the present Mr. Van Dorn has a somewhat clouded claim to the acreage.

Van. My father's title was clear, and he left it to me.

Skimmerhorn. The truth is he should have employed a lawyer when he drew his will, because the instrument, as recorded, is faulty in many respects. It was brought before me in my capacity as probate judge at Ledentown.

Van. And in your capacity as second vice-president of the trap-rock company you shot it full of holes.

Skimmerhorn. Sir, I keep my duties entirely separate.

Van. Sure, but when your left hand takes money your right hand finds out about it. And when there's too much to carry away in both hands you use a basket. You're also vice-president of the power company, and

you stole right-of-ways clear across the county north and
south—

Skimmerhorn. We paid for every foot of land—

Van. Yes, at your own price.

Biggs. Let's not get in an argument, Mr. Van Dorn, because the fact that your father's will was improperly
drawn means he died intestate and the land goes to
his heirs. Now we've found twenty-seven Van Dorns
living at Blauvelt, all claiming relationship and all will-
ing to sign away their rights for a consideration.

Van. The best you can do you'll need my name in your
little paper, and you won't have it.

Skimmerhorn. To put it straight, you'll take three thousand dollars, and I'll hold the will valid.

Van. Oh, it's three thousand, now?

Biggs. You'll say that's crooked, but it's not. It's perfectly
legal—and it's what you get.

Van. I'm still waiting to hear what you do about my sig-
nature.

Skimmerhorn. It's quite possible you'll be held incompetent by the court and a guardian appointed.

Van. Me, incompetent.

Skimmerhorn. But I've got the validation in my pocket,
naming you executor, if you'll sell.

Biggs. And by God, anybody that won't take money when
it's offered to him is incompetent! And you'll take it

now or not at all! I don't go mountain-climbing every
day with a blank check in my pocket!

[*A pause*]

Come on: It's bad enough sliding down that trail by
daylight.

Van. Well, I wouldn't want to make you nervous,
a couple of eminent respectables
like you two—but a dog won't bite a Dutchman—
maybe you've heard that—and the reason is
a Dutchman's poison when he don't like you. Now,
I'm Dutch and I don't like you.

Skimmerhorn. That's a threat?

Van. Not at all. Only don't try to eat me
or you'll curl up. I'm poison to a hound-dog,
and you're both sons-of-bitches.

Biggs. Come on.

[*The daylight is now gone. The airplane beacon lights the scene
from the right.*]

Van. What's more
there's something funny about this mountain-top.
It draws fire. Every storm on the Tappan Zee
climbs up here and wraps itself around
High Tor, and blazes away at what you've got,
airplane beacon, steam-shovels, anything
newfangled. It smashed the beacon twice. It blew
the fuses on your shovel and killed a man
only last week. I've got a premonition
something might happen to you.

Biggs. God, he's crazy.

Skimmerhorn. Yeah, let him talk.
> [*There is a sudden rumbling roar of falling rock.*]

Biggs. What's that?

Van. That's nothing much.
That's just a section of the cliff come down
across the trail. I've been expecting it
this last two years. You'd better go down this way.

Biggs. This way?

Van. Yeah.

Biggs. No, thanks.

Van. Just as you say.
But there's something definitely hostile here
toward you two pirates. Don't try that trail in the dark.
Not if you want to be buried in your vaults
in Mount Repose. Your grieving families
might have to move two thousand tons of rock
to locate your remains. You think High Tor's
just so much raw material, but you're wrong.
A lot of stubborn men have died up here
and some of them don't sleep well. They come back
and push things round, these dark nights. Don't blame
                    me
if anything falls on you.

Skimmerhorn. Oh, what the hell!
Let's get out of here.
> [*Another long rumble of falling rock*]

Van. Another rock-fall.
Once they start there's likely to be more.
Something hanging round in the dark up here

doesn't like you boys. Not only me.
Better go down this way.

Biggs. Thanks.

[BIGGS *and* SKIMMERHORN *go out to the right.*]

Judith. What do you mean?

Van. I don't know.

Judith. They'll say you threatened them.
Good-bye, Van.

Van. You'll be up tomorrow?

Judith. No.

[*She steps down into a cleft.*]

Van. You'd better let me see you down.

Judith. Oh, no.
I can climb. Stay here and guard your rock—
you think so much of it.

Van. When will I see you?

Judith. Never.
We'll forget about it. You had a choice
and you chose High Tor. You're in love with your
mountain.
Well, keep your mountain.

Van. All right.

Judith. Good night.

Van. Good night.

[*She disappears down the rocks.* VAN *sits in the shadow, looking into darkness. After a moment a barely perceptible
*FIGURE *enters from the gloom at the right and crosses the*

1 41 74

stage toward the rocks at the left. At the foot of the climb he pauses and his face is caught in the light of the beacon. He is seen to be young or middle-aged, bearded, and wearing the costume of a Dutch sailor of the sixteen hundreds. He climbs the rocks, and ANOTHER SAILOR, *a small cask strapped to his shoulders, follows.* THREE MORE *cross the stage similarly, then the* CAPTAIN *and* HIS WIFE *pause, like the others, in the light of the beacon. The* CAPTAIN *is like his men, only younger perhaps;* HIS WIFE *is a tiny figure, with a delicate girlish face looking out from under the Dutch bonnet. They too pass up the rocks, and are followed by a rolling* SILENUS *in the same garments. As they vanish* VAN *rises, looking after them.*]

Uh—huh—going to rain.

CURTAIN

ACT ONE

Scene II

SCENE: *The curtain goes up on complete darkness enfolding the summit of the Tor. There is a long cumbrous rolling, as of a ball going down a bowling alley, a flash of white light, a crackling as of falling pins and a mutter dying into echo along the hills. The flash reveals the outline of the Tor, black against the sky, and on it the figures of the* DUTCH CREW. *Again the roll, the flash, the break and the dying away. The beam of the airplane beacon steals into the scene sufficiently to suggest the bowlers, some of them standing, some sitting about the keg, the* CAPTAIN'S WIFE *a little apart from the rest. Beyond the peak is a moving floor, the upper side of blown cloud.*

The Captain's Wife. I'm weary of it, Martin! When you drink
there should be one on guard to watch the river
lest the ship come, and pass, and we must haunt
the dark another year!

The Captain. To humor her,
Pieter, old son, climb down and post the Zee,
and mind you keep good lookout.

Pieter. Ships, aye, ships—
when the ball's rolling and there's gin in hand
I go to post. My luck!

The Captain. When you shipped with me
you signed the voyage.

Pieter. Is this sea or land?
I'm no foot soldier!

The Captain. March!

27

Pieter. Aye, aye. I'm going.

> [PIETER *detaches himself from the group and goes down the rocks.*]

The Captain. Are you content?

The Captain's Wife. When the *Half Moon* returns
and we have boarded her, and the wind scuds fair
into the east—yes, when we see the wharves
of Texel town across the Zuyder Zee,
with faces waiting for us, hands and cries
to welcome our returning, then perhaps
I shall be content.

A Sailor. Now God, for Texel town.

Another Soldier.

> [*Rising*]

I'll drink no more.

DeWitt.

> [*The Silenus*]

Drink up, lads, and forget.
It's a long way to the Texel. Drink your drink
and play your play.

The Captain. Drink up and play it out.

The Captain's Wife. Have you forgotten how the cobbled
street
comes down by cranks and turns upon the quay,
where the *Onrust* set sail? The traders' doors
under the blowing signs, bright colors hung
to catch unwary eyes? The bakers' ovens
and the long, hot brown loaves? The red-coal fires
and silver under candles? There your wives

wait for you, their sharp roofs in Amsterdam
cut on a rainy sky.

The Captain. Be quiet, Lise.
You were so much in love you must come with me;
you were so young that I was patient with you,
but now day long, night long you carp and quarrel,
a carping wife.

Lise. We stay so long—so long;
Asher, at first the days were years, but now
the years are days; the ship that set us down
to watch this river palisade becomes
alike with supper-stories round a hearth
when we were children. Was there this ship at all,
was there a sailor-city, Amsterdam,
where the salt water washed the shallow piers
and the wind went out to sea? Will the ship return,
and shall I then see the Netherlands once more,
with sabots clattering homeward from the school
on winter evenings?

Asher. Aye, there was a ship,
and we wait here for her, but she's long away,
somewhere up-river.

Lise. And now you drink and drink,
distill your liquor on the mountain-top
and bowl against the light. But when you break it
these new strange men come build it up again;
and giant shovels spade the mountain down,
and when you break them still the new strange men
rig them afresh and turn them on the rock,
eating the pillared stone. We must go back.
There's no safety here.

A Sailor. We must go back.

Asher. These muttering fools!

Lise. Oh, Asher, I'm afraid!
　　For one thing I have known, and never told
　　lest it be true, lest you be frightened, too,
　　lest we be woven of shadow! As the years
　　have gone, each year a century, they seem
　　less real, and all the boundaries of time,
　　our days and nights and hours, merge and are one,
　　escaping me. Then sometimes in a morning
　　when all the crew come down the rocks together,
　　holding my breath, I see you in the light,
　　and back of you the gray rock bright and hard,
　　seen through figures of air! And you, and you,
　　and you were but cloud-drift walking, pierced by the
　　　　　　　　　　　　light,
　　translucent in the sun.

DeWitt. Now damn the woman!

Lise. Love, love, before our blood
　　be shadow only, in a dark fairyland
　　so far from home, we must go back, go back
　　where earth is earth, and we may live again
　　and one day be one day!

Asher. Why, then, I knew it,
　　and I have known it, now that you know it, too.
　　But the old Amsterdam of our farewells
　　lies in another world. The land and sea
　　about us on this dark side of the earth
　　is thick with demons, heavy with enchantment,
　　cutting us off from home.

Lise. Is it enchantment?
    Yes, it may be. At home there were tulips growing
    along my bordered path, but here the flowers
    are strange to me, not one I knew, no trace
    of any flower I knew; no, seedlings set
    upon a darkened, alien outer rim
    of sea, blown here as we were blown, enchanted,
    drunken and blind with sorcery.

Asher. And yet
    what we're to have we shall have here. Years past
    the demons of this air palsied our hands,
    fixed us upon one pinnacle of time,
    and on this pinnacle of stone, and all
    the world we knew slid backward to the gulf,
    stranding us here like seaweed on the shingle,
    remembering the sea. In Texel town
    new houses have gone up, after new fashions;
    the children of the children of our days,
    lying awake to think of what has been,
    reach doubtfully beyond the clouds of years
    back to our sailing out of Texel. Men
    are like the gods, work miracles, have power
    to pierce the walls with music. Their beacon light
    destroys us. You have seen us in the sun,
    wraithlike, half-effaced, the print we make
    upon the air thin tracery, permeable,
    a web of wind. They have changed us. We may take
    the fire-balls of the lightning in our hands
    and bowl them down the level floor of cloud
    to wreck the beacon, yet there was a time
    when these were death to touch. The life we keep
    is motionless as the center of a storm,

yet while we can we keep it; while we can
snuff out to darkness their bright sweeping light,
melt down the harness of the slow machines
that hew the mountain from us. When it goes
we shall go too. They leave us this place, High Tor,
and we shall have no other. You learn it last.
A long while now we've known.

A Sailor. Aye, aye, a long while.

Asher. Come, we'll go down.

> [*The* CAPTAIN *and his* MEN *go out, leaving only* DEWITT *with*
> LISE.]

Lise. That's why they drink.

DeWitt. It's enough to drive a sailor-man to drink, by the
great jib boom, marooned somewhere on the hinder
parts of the earth and degenerating hourly to the status
of a flying Dutchman, half-spook and half God-knows-
what. Maps and charts we have, compass and sextant,
but the ships these days are bewitched like ourselves,
spanking up and down the Mauritius with sails struck,
against wind and tide, and on fire from below. Drink?
Why wouldn't we drink? A pewter flagon of Hollands
gin puts manhood into the remnants and gives a sailor
courage to look out on these fanciful new devils that
ride sea, land and air on a puff of blue smoke. They're
all witches and mermaids, these new-world devils, dancing around on bubbles, speaking a language God never
heard, and nothing human about them except when
they fall they break like the rest of us.

Lise. If I had known. It's not too late. The sun
still rises in the east and lays a course

toward the old streets and days. These are my hands
as when I was a child. Some great magician,
binding a half-world in his wiles, has laid
a spell here. We must break it and go home.
I see this clearly.

DeWitt. Lise, little heart, the devils are too much for us.
God knows it's a hard thing to say, and I'd help you
if I could help myself, but all hell wouldn't know
where we are nor where we ought to go. The very
points of the compass grow doubtful these latter years,
partly because I'm none too sober and partly because
the great master devil sits on top of the world stirring
up north and south with a long spoon to confuse poor
mariners. I've seen him at it, a horned bull three times
the size of Dundenberg and with more cloven feet than
the nine beasts in Revelations. Very clearly I saw him,
too, as clear as you see the east and a path across the
waters.

Lise. Are we to wait till all the color steals
from flower and cloud, before our eyes; till a wind
out of the morning from the Tappan Zee
lifts us, we are so light, for all our crying,
and takes us down the valleys toward the west,
and all we are becomes a voiceless cry
heard on the wind?

DeWitt. We'll see the time, if they continue to work on
us, when we'll be apparent in a strong light only by
the gin contained in our interior piping. The odor itself, along with that of church-warden tobacco, should
be sufficient to convince a magistrate of our existence.—
You tremble, little Lise, and you weep, but look now,

there's a remedy I've had in mind. Fall in love with
one of them. Fall in love with one of these same strange
new-world magicians. I shall choose me out one of their
female mermaid witches, and set my heart on her, and
become a man again. And for God's sake let her love me
strongly and hold on, lest I go down the brook like a
spring freshet in the next pounding rain.

Lise. I gave my love long ago, and it's no help.
I love enough.

DeWitt. Aye, but he's in a worse case than you are, the
Captain. Saving his captaincy, there's not enough be-
lief in him to produce half a tear in a passion of
sobbing. You'll make me weep, little one, and what
tears I have I shall need, lest my protestation turns out
to be a dry rain.

Lise. Aye, we were warned before we came away
against the cabalistic words and signs
of those who dwell along these unknown waters;
never to watch them dance nor hear them sing
nor draw their imprecations—lest their powers
weave a weird medicine throughout the air,
chilling the blood, transfixing body and mind
and we be chained invisibly, our eyes darkened,
our wrists and breasts pulseless, anchored in time,
like birds blown back in a wind. But we have listened,
and we are stricken through with light and sound,
empty as autumn leaves, empty as prayers
that drift in a godless heaven. Meaningless,
picked clean of meaning, stripped of bone and will,
the chrysalids of locusts staring here
at one another.

DeWitt. If it's true it's enough to make a man weep for himself, Lise, and for all lost mariners, wherever they are, and for us more than any, here on these spell-bound rocks, drawing up water from time past—the well growing deeper, and the water lower, till there be none.

[*He turns away to go down the path.*]

CURTAIN

ACT ONE

Scene III

SCENE: *Another section of the Tor, in darkness save for the airplane beacon. A large steam shovel reaches in from an adjacent excavation and hangs over the rock, the control cables dangling. VAN is alone on the stage looking at the machinery. He reaches up, catches a cable, and swings the shovel a little. BIGGS and SKIMMERHORN enter from the right.*

Biggs. Hey, what are you doing with that shovel?

Van. Did you know you're trespassing? Also when a man owns land he owns the air above it and the rock below. That means this damn shovel of yours is also trespassing.

Biggs. Oh, it's Van Dorn. We'll have that moved tomorrow, Mr. Van Dorn. Somebody's made a miscue and left it hanging over the line.

Skimmerhorn. By the way, that trail's gone out completely, Mr. Van Dorn; there's a fifty foot sheer drop there now, where it was. Now we've got to get off, if you can think of any way to manage it.

Van. I'm not worrying about it. Spend the night. No charge.

Skimmerhorn. The truth is I have to be in court early tomorrow, and a man needs his sleep.

Van. Afraid you'd doze off on the bench and somebody else might take a trick? Oh, you'd wake up before they got far with anything. The Skimmerhorns are automatic that way.

Biggs. You don't know any other trail down?

Van. I showed you the one I knew, and you both turned green looking at it. What am I supposed to do now? Pin wings on you?
   [*He goes out to the right.*]

Skimmerhorn. I think I'll swear out a warrant for that squirt. He's too independent by half.

Biggs. On what ground?

Skimmerhorn. He threatened us, didn't he?

Biggs. And where'll that get us?

Skimmerhorn. He might be easier to talk to in jail.

Biggs. That's true.

Skimmerhorn.
   [*Sitting on a rock*]
   This is a hell of a mess.

Biggs. You're explaining to me?

Skimmerhorn. What did we ever come up here for?

Biggs. Twenty-two thousand dollars.

Skimmerhorn. Will we get it?

Biggs. It'll look all right on the books.

Skimmerhorn. It's not good enough, though.

Biggs. What are you grousing about?

Skimmerhorn. Because I want my dinner, damn it! And because I'm tired of taking forty per cent and giving you sixty on all the side bets! I want half!

Biggs. You're a damn sight more likely to get your dinner. You're overpaid already.

Skimmerhorn. The will's perfectly good. I could find holes in it, but I've probated plenty much the same.

Biggs. What of it?

Skimmerhorn. A judge has some conscience, you know. When he sets a precedent he likes to stick to it.

Biggs. I never knew your conscience to operate except on a cash basis. You want half.

Skimmerhorn. Yes, I want half.

Biggs. Well, you don't get it. Any other judge I put in there'd work for nothing but the salary and glad of the job. You take a forty per cent cut and howl for more. The woods are full of shyster lawyers looking for probate judgeships and I'll slip one in at Ledentown next election.

Skimmerhorn. Oh, no, you won't, Art; oh, no, you won't. You wouldn't do that to an old friend like me; because if you did, think what I'd do to an old friend like you.

Biggs. Well, maybe I wouldn't. Not if you're reasonable. Look, what's the difference between forty per cent and fifty per cent? Practically nothing!

Skimmerhorn. Then why don't you give it to me?

Biggs. Because, try and get it!—

Skimmerhorn. Damn it, I'm hungry.—I ought to telephone my wife, too.

Biggs. Why don't you?

Skimmerhorn. Maybe it's fun for you—nothing to eat, no place to sleep, cold as hell, black as Tophet and a storm coming up! Only I'm not used to it!

Biggs. You're pulling down forty per cent of twenty-two thousand dollars for the night's work. I say it's worth it.

Skimmerhorn. Think we could slide down one of those cables?

Biggs. Maybe you could, Humpty-Dumpty, but not me.

Skimmerhorn. I'm going to look at it.

[*He goes out left,* BIGGS *following. After a moment* THREE MEN *climb in through the rocks at the right, one of them carrying a small zipper satchel. They throw themselves down wearily on the rock. They are, in brief, the Nanuet bank robbers,* ELKUS, DOPE *and* BUDDY.]

Dope. God, I got no wind.

[*A siren is heard faintly, far down on the road.*]

Elkus. Sons a' bitches a' troopers.

Dope. What'd you want to wreck the car for?

Elkus. Want to get caught with the stuff on you?

Buddy. We'll get four hundred years for this.

Elkus. Shut up!

Dope. You didn't need to wreck the car, though.

Elkus. Didn't you hear the trooper slam on the brakes when he went by? You'd be wearing bracelets right now if I hadn't dumped the old crate over the embankment! The way it is he thinks he's following us, and he'll blow that fire alarm all the way to Bear Mountain

Bridge. Only hope he meets something solid head-on at ninety miles an hour.

Dope. What I want to know is where we go from here.

Elkus. Down the other side and pick up a car.
[*The siren is heard receding.*]

Buddy. We'll get four hundred years for this.

Elkus. What do you think you are, a chorus? Go on back to St. Thomas's and sing it to the priest. You're about as much help as a flat tire.

Buddy. I never wanted to be in it. I was only lookout— you're both witness to that.

Elkus. What good do you think that does you, you poor fish? Brace up and take it like a man. There's twenty-five thousand in that bag and some of it's yours.

Dope. How do you know it's twenty-five thousand?

Elkus. It's the Orangeburg pay roll.
[BUDDY *looks off left.*]

Buddy. Before God, it's Judge Skimmerhorn!

Elkus. What? Where?

Buddy. There. Coming round the rocks. Judge Skimmerhorn of Ledentown.

Elkus. Does he know you?

Buddy. Sure, he knows me.

Elkus. We're out climbing, see? Hikers, see? On a picnic.
[*They stand.* ELKUS *holds the satchel behind him casually.* BIGGS *and* SKIMMERHORN *come in.*]

Biggs. Hello.

Elkus. How are you?

Biggs. Out walking?

Elkus. That's right. Climbed up on a bet.

Skimmerhorn. Isn't that Buddy?

Buddy. Yes, sir. Evening, Judge.

Skimmerhorn. You're a long way from home.

Buddy. Yes, sir.

Biggs. Think you could show us a way down? We're stuck up here.

Buddy. There's a path down the cliff. Yes, sir.

Skimmerhorn. No, thanks. I saw that one. Going to camp here?

Elkus. Might as well. Sure.

Skimmerhorn. Bring anything to eat?

Elkus. Matter of fact, we didn't.
  [*He sets the satchel down behind the rock, unobtrusively.*]

Skimmerhorn. Not a thing?

Elkus. Not a thing.

Skimmerhorn. That's funny. Camping with nothing to eat.

Elkus. Yeah, it is kinda funny.

Dope. We ate before we started.
  [*He smiles cunningly.*]

Elkus. That's right. The Dope's right for once. We ate before we started.

Skimmerhorn. Wish I had.

Buddy. You—you staying up here tonight, sir?

Skimmerhorn. Seems that way. We came up looking for somebody.

Elkus. Looking for somebody?

Skimmerhorn. That's what I said.

Elkus. Who was it?

Biggs. That's our business.

Elkus. I see.

Skimmerhorn.

[*Coming near the three*]

Listen, Buddy, you're young and ambitious. Would you do something for me if you got well paid?

Buddy. I guess so, Judge.

Skimmerhorn.

[*Sitting on the rock and incidentally over the satchel*]

We're done in, traipsing around the rocks. Would you climb down the Tor and get to Haverstraw and telephone my wife I can't come home?

Buddy. I guess so, wouldn't I, Elkus?

Elkus. Up to you.

Skimmerhorn. And while you're there will you buy a dozen sandwiches and some beer?

Buddy. Yes, sir.

Skimmerhorn. There's another thing you could do. Call up the state troopers for me, and tell them I'm here and I want them to come up and make an arrest.

Buddy. You—want to arrest somebody?

Skimmerhorn. You get it. What do you say?

Buddy. I—I guess so. Is it all right, Elkus?

Dope. Oh—no. Oh—no.

Elkus. Sure it's O.K. Why not?

Buddy. It'd take about five hours—to get down and back.

Skimmerhorn. Damn it—I'll starve to death.

Dope. What do you want to make an arrest for?

Biggs. That's our business.

Buddy. All right. I'll go.

Skimmerhorn. Here's five dollars for you. And another when you get back. And make it fast, will you?

Buddy. Yes, sir.
　[*He starts out right.*]

Elkus. Just a minute, Bud.
　[ELKUS *and* DOPE *follow* BUDDY *out to converse with him.*]

Biggs. You might have made it two dozen sandwiches.

Skimmerhorn. I guess I will.
　[*He starts to rise, places his hand on the satchel, and jumps.*]
　Christ, what's that?
　[*He kicks the satchel, then flips it up into the rocks.*]

Biggs. Yeah?

Skimmerhorn. I thought it was a snake. Somebody's mouldy luggage. People are always throwing truck around.

[*He calls.*]

Say, for God's sake, get started, will you?

Buddy.

[*Outside*]

Yes, sir. Right away.

[ELKUS *and* DOPE *return.*]

Elkus. I guess we'll all go.

[*He looks nonchalantly where the satchel was.*]

Skimmerhorn. Fine. Will you make it two dozen sandwiches?

Elkus. What the hell's going on here?

Skimmerhorn. We're hungry, that's all.

Elkus. Are you two finnegling with us? Because if you are—!

Biggs. What are you looking for?

Elkus. Nothing. Who said I was looking for anything?

Dope. Hey, Elkus! They got the troopers up here!

[DEWITT's *broad Dutch hat appears above the rocks in the rear, looking, for the moment, remarkably like that of a state trooper.* ELKUS *and* DOPE *freeze, looking at it.*]

Elkus.

[*Drawing a gun*]

Why, you fat pimps!
[DeWitt *disappears*.]

Dope. Beat it, you fool!
[Elkus *and* Dope *scatter out to the right*.]

Biggs.
[*Looking at the rocks*]

What was all that about?

Skimmerhorn. I hope they bring those sandwiches.
[*He also stares toward the rear*.]

Biggs. Sandwiches? They're not bringing sandwiches for anybody, those two.
[*He calls*.]

Hey! Hey, you! Anybody there?—What did he mean by troopers?

Skimmerhorn. Want to take a look?

Biggs. I'm plenty unhappy, right where I am.
[Skimmerhorn *climbs up on the rocks*.]

Skimmerhorn. Wish to God I did see a trooper.

Biggs. Nobody there?

Skimmerhorn. Not a thing. Hey! Hey, you!
[*A silence*.]

Nope. Nobody.

Biggs. Looks to me as if we just missed being stuck up by a couple of lunatics.

Skimmerhorn. If I can't eat I'm going to sleep.

Biggs. Maybe you've never tried adjusting yourself to igneous limestone.

Skimmerhorn. I'm about to try it now.

Biggs. You have my sympathy.

> [SKIMMERHORN *stretches out on the rock, takes off his coat for a pillow and lies down.*]

Skimmerhorn. Thanks.

Biggs. Beautiful shape you have. A lot of slop tied up with a piece of string.

Skimmerhorn.

> [*Sitting up*]

God it's cold. Listen, we could use one coat for a pillow and put the other one over us.

Biggs. What other one?

Skimmerhorn. Yours.

Biggs. A proposition, huh?

Skimmerhorn. You going to sit up all night?

Biggs. In some ways it might be preferable.

Skimmerhorn. You can't prop yourself on end forever, like a duck on a rock.

Biggs. Pull yourself together, then. You stick out behind like a bump on a duck. All right. Move over.

Skimmerhorn. Your coat's bigger than mine.

> [*They pull* BIGGS' *coat around them and lie down.*]

Biggs. Just a couple of perfect forty-nines. Where the hell am I supposed to put my hip bone?

Skimmerhorn. You juggle your own hip bones.

> [DEWITT *appears on the rocks at the rear, looking down.*]

Biggs. If you snore, you probate judge, I'll have you disbarred.

Skimmerhorn. Go to sleep.

Biggs. Wish I thought I could. On bed rock. Wake me early, mother dear.

Skimmerhorn. Shut up.

> [DEWITT *meanwhile has opened the satchel and now brings it down into the light to examine the contents. He sits down, takes out five packets of bills, shakes the satchel, then begins to go through the inner pockets. He finds a roll of pennies, which he breaks open into his hands.*]

DeWitt. Copper pieces, by the great jib boom, enough to purchase a new wig, if a man ever got back to a place where money was useful to him. A counting-house full of them wouldn't buy a ship from one of these semi-demi-demi-semi-devils, so that's no good.

> [*Two snores rise in concert from* BIGGS *and* SKIMMERHORN. DE-WITT *goes over to them, dropping the money.*]

What kind of demi-semi-devil do you think you are, with four legs and two faces, both looking the same direction? Jesu Maria, it's a kind of centaur, as big one way as another, no arms, and feet the size of dishpans.

Biggs. What's that?

DeWitt.

[*Backing away*]

It's the rear end that talks, evidently, the front being fast asleep in the manner of a figure-head.

Biggs. Who's there? Did somebody speak?

DeWitt. None too clear in the back thinker, I should say, which would be a natural result of lugging two sets of brains, fore and aft. I'd incline to communicate with the front end, but if necessary I'll converse with the posterior.

Biggs.

[*Sitting up, looking at* DeWitt]

Skimmerhorn!

Skimmerhorn. What's the matter?

Biggs. I'm damned if I know.

Skimmerhorn. Go to sleep, then.

Biggs. Do you believe in apparitions?

Skimmerhorn. No.

Biggs. Well, there's a figure of fun sitting talking to me, right out of a masquerade ball.

Skimmerhorn. You been drinking?

Biggs. What would I find to drink?

DeWitt. If the forecastle wakes now I shall play both ends against the middle, like a marine auctioneer. I want to buy a boat.

Biggs. You've come to the wrong shop, sailor. I'm in the real-estate business, and it's a long mile down to sea level.

[SKIMMERHORN *sits up suddenly.*]

DeWitt. You have no boats?

Biggs. No boats.

Skimmerhorn. What in the hell?—

Biggs. I told you I'm damned if I know.

DeWitt. And the front end has no boats?

Biggs. You're the front end, see. He wants to know if you've got boats.

Skimmerhorn. No, stranger, no boats.

DeWitt. Ah.

[*He shakes his head mournfully, turns him about and goes to the right, still muttering.*]

The great plague on them, the lying, two-headed fairies out of a witch's placket. What chance has an honest man against a two-faced double-tongued beast, telling the same tale—

[*He disappears through the rocks.*]

Biggs. Did you see what I saw?

Skimmerhorn. Not if you saw what I saw. What I saw wasn't possible.—Did you fake that thing?

Biggs. Fake it? I saw it.

Skimmerhorn. Oh, no—! Nobody saw that—what I saw. I didn't either. I've got a family to support. They aren't going to put me away anywhere.

Biggs. Whatever it was, it left a calling card. Looks as if he ate his lunch here, supposing a thing like that eats lunch. Maybe he left some for us.

Skimmerhorn. I don't want any of that.

Biggs.
　　[*Rising and turning the packages over with his foot*]

There's something in it.

Skimmerhorn. Help yourself.

Biggs.
　　[*Opening a package, tossing the cover away*]

You know what this is?

Skimmerhorn. Probably a sheaf of contracts with the devil, all ready to sign.

Biggs. No, it's money.

Skimmerhorn. Money!
　　[*He leaps to his feet.*]

Biggs. Fives and tens.
　　[*He opens another package.* Skimmerhorn *does the same.*]

Skimmerhorn. Well, bless the poor little Dutchman's heart—after all we said about him, too!

Biggs. Think he left it?

Skimmerhorn. It wasn't there before.

Biggs. No.

Skimmerhorn. Were you born with a caul, or anything?

Biggs. Always before I had to work for it, or steal it. Never till tonight have I been waked up by a little man in a big hat, fetching it to me in packages.

Skimmerhorn. Are you asleep?

Biggs. I probably am, asleep and dreaming.

Skimmerhorn. If you're dreaming, you're dreaming that I found money.

Biggs. Oh, you found it now?

Skimmerhorn. Fifty-fifty.

Biggs. Wait a minute. You know what money this is?

Skimmerhorn. No.
　　[BIGGS *picks up a discarded envelope.*]

Biggs. It came out of the Nanuet bank.
　　[SKIMMERHORN *takes the envelope from him.*]

Skimmerhorn. If that little guy's a bank robber he's certainly careless with the proceeds.

Biggs. That's where it came from.

Skimmerhorn. In that case we ought to give it back. For the reward.

Biggs. No reward offered yet.

Skimmerhorn. Maybe we ought to give it back anyway.

Biggs. Think so?

Skimmerhorn. Might be marked bills.

Biggs. No, it's not. I was talking with the president of the bank on the 'phone. Made up for a pay roll. No marks on any of it.

Skimmerhorn. It ought to be returned, though.

Biggs. Sure, it should. Question is, will it be?

Skimmerhorn. I think so, don't you?

Biggs. I'm inclined to think so. Bank robbing's away out of my line.

Skimmerhorn. Mine, too, as a matter of fact. The president of the bank's a friend of yours?

Biggs. Yes, he is, in a way. Oh, he's gypped me a couple of times, same as you would.

Skimmerhorn. He wouldn't lose anything.

Biggs. Oh, no, he's insured.

Skimmerhorn. Has it occurred to you the little Dutchman that was here might not mean any good to us?

Biggs. Did you see a little Dutchman?

Skimmerhorn. I thought I did, there for a minute.

Biggs. I don't believe that any more.

Skimmerhorn. Certainly doesn't sound very likely.

Biggs. We'd better count it. Man never ought to carry money around without knowing how much it is.

Skimmerhorn. Yeah, let's count it. It said twenty-five thousand in the paper.

Biggs. You know, nobody in the world would ever know who had it?

Skimmerhorn. No, they wouldn't.

Biggs. What do you say?

Skimmerhorn. I say fifty-fifty.

Biggs. Damn you, Skimmerhorn, if I hadn't been in business with you for twenty years I'd say you were a crook!

Skimmerhorn. If I wasn't a crook after twenty years with you I'd be slow in the head and hard of hearing!

Biggs. What's fifty per cent of twenty-five thousand? Twelve thousand five hundred? And what's forty per cent? Ten thousand! Are you going to hold up the deal for two thousand five hundred?

Skimmerhorn. I certainly am.

Biggs. All right, take it. Fifty-fifty on this one deal.

Skimmerhorn. And on the Van Dorn deal, too.

Biggs. Why, you fat louse—
> [VAN DORN *comes in from the right out of the shadows.*]

Van. Sorry to bother you gentlemen, but—

Biggs.
> [*As they stuff the bills into their pockets*]

Where the hell did you come from?

Van. Why, you're not friends of mine, but there's a storm blowing in and it occurred to me I might show you where you could keep dry under a ledge.

Biggs. Thanks. Much obliged.

Van. Want me to go with you?

Biggs. No, thanks—Let's get a little nearer the light.

Skimmerhorn. Good idea.

> [BIGGS *and* SKIMMERHORN *go out right.* VAN *looks after them, then picks up one of the discarded envelopes and studies it. He sits.* LISE *comes up the rocks in the rear and stands looking out to the river, shading her eyes from the beacon.*]

Lise. You who have watched this river in the past
  till your hope turned bitterness, pity me now,
  my hope gone, but no power to keep my eyes
  from the mocking water. The hills come down like
                    sand,
  and the long barges bear them off to town,
  to what strange market in what stranger town,
  devouring mountains? but never, in all days,
  never, though I should watch here without rest,
  will any ship come downward with the tide
  flying the flag we knew.

> [VAN *rises.* LISE *draws back an instant, then comes down a step toward him.*]

  Do you hear my voice?

Van. Yes, lady.

Lise. Do you see me in the light,
  as I see you?

Van. Yes.

Lise. You are one of those
  the earth bears now, the quick, fierce wizard men
  who plow the mountains down with steel, and set
  new mountains in their sky. You've come to drive
  machines through the white rock's heart.

Van. Not I. I haven't.
  I hate them all like poison.

Lise. You're against them—
the great machines?

Van. I'd like to smash the lot,
and the men that own them.

Lise. Oh, if there were a friend
among so many enemies! I wish
I knew how to make you friend. But now my voice
shrinks back in me, reluctant, a cold thing,
fearing the void between us.—I have seen you.
I know you. You are kind.

Van. How do you know?

Lise. When I have been most lonely in the spring,
the spring rain beating with my heart, I made
a wild flower garden; none of these I knew,
for none I knew are here, flowers of the woods,
little and lovely, nameless. One there was
like a pink moccasin, another low
with blotted leaves, wolf-toothed, and many more
rooted among the fern. I saw you then
come on this garden, secret as the tears
wept for lost days, and drew my breath in dread
that you should laugh and trample it. You smiled
and then went on. But when I came again
there was a new flower growing with the rest,
one I'd not seen. You brought and placed it there
only for love of gardens, ignorant whose
the garden you enriched. What was this flower?

Van. Wild orchid. It was your garden?

Lise. Yes. You know
the names of all the flowers?

Van. Yes.

Lise. But then
　　you'd teach them to me?

Van. Yes.

Lise. Teach me the names.
　　What is the tall three-petaled one that's black
　　almost, the red's so dark?

Van. That's trillium.
　　Speaking of flowers, tell me your name.

Lise. It's Lise,
　　or used to be.

Van. Not now?

Lise. I'm weary of it,
　　and all things that I've been. You have a lover?
　　She'll be angry?

Van. She's angry now. She's off
　　and gone. She won't come back.

Lise. Love me a little,
　　enough to save me from the dark. But if
　　you cannot give me love, find me a way!
　　The seas lie black between your harbor town
　　and mine, but your ships are quick. If I might see
　　the corner where the three streets come to an end
　　on sundial windows, there, a child by a fire—
　　no, but it's gone!

Van. I've seen you on the hills
　　moving with shadows. But you're not shadow.

Lise. No.
 Could one live and be shadow?

Van. Take my hand.

Lise. I dare not.

Van. Come, let me see your garden.

Lise. No.
 I dare not. It is your race that thins our blood
 and gathers round, besieging us with charms
 to stay the feet of years. But I know you kind.—
 Love me a little. Never put out your hand
 to touch me, lest some magic in your blood
 reach me, and I be nothing. What I am
 I know not, under these spells, if I be cloud
 or dust. Nor whether you dream of me, or I
 make you of light and sound. Between this stone
 and the near constellations of the stars
 I go and come, doubting now whence I come
 or when I go. Cling to me. Keep me still.
 Be gentle. You were gentle with the orchid—
 Take my hand now.

Van. You're cold.

Lise. Yes.

Van. Here on the Tor
 the sun beats down like murder all day long
 and the wind comes up like murder in the night.
 I'm cold myself.

Lise. How have I slipped so far
 from the things you have? I'm puzzled here and lost.
 Is it so different for you? Keep my hand

and tell me. In these new times are all men shadow?
All men lost?

Van. Sometimes I stand here at night
and look out over the river when a fog
covers the lights. Then if it's dark enough
and I can't see my hands or where the rock
leaves off against the cloud, and I'm alone,
then, well I'm damned if I know who I am,
staring out into that black. Maybe I'm cloud
and maybe I'm dust. I might be old as time.
I'd like to think I knew. A man gets that way
standing staring at darkness.

Lise. Then—you do know.
It's better now.—Somewhere along a verge
where your life dips in dusk and my gray days
lift to the light a moment, we walk there
and our eyes meet.—Look, when the wizards come
to tear the mountain down, I'll have no place.
I'll be gone then.

Van. Child, they won't get our mountain!
Not if I have to shoot them as they come
they won't get our mountain! The mountain's mine,
and you're to make your garden where you like;
their feet won't step across it! All their world's
made up of fat men doing tricks with laws
to manage tides and root up hills. The hills
can afford to laugh at them! A race of grubs
bred down from men!

Lise. Is it the light I feel
come flooding back in me? Light or their charms
broken here, seeing your face?

Van. Your hands are warm.

Lise. I'm not cold now; for an instant I'm not cold,
seeing your face. This is your wizardry.
Let me stand here and see you.

Elkus.
    [*Outside*]

Somewhere around here it was. Over toward the crane.

Dope.
    [*Outside*]

What'd you go and put down the satchel for?

Elkus.
    [*Outside*]

How did I know he'd sit on top of it?
    [VAN *and* LISE *slip out through the rocks at the rear.* ELKUS *and*
    DOPE *come in furtively from the right.*]

Dope. That's where. Under that rock.

Elkus. Keep your eye peeled. They're probably beating
the woods for us.

Dope. What's that?
    [*He picks up an envelope.*]

Elkus. They got it.

Dope. God damn the rotten business! Now we will get
four hundred years.

Elkus. Now you're saying it—

Dope. What are we going to do?

Elkus. I'm going to send Buddy back with sandwiches to
see if the Judge got the money. If he did we'll stick
him up.

Dope. Hey, how about the troopers?

Elkus. If that was troopers I'm Admiral Dewey. Troopers would a' used the artillery. Come on.

Dope. O.K. Some pennies here.

Elkus. To hell with 'em.

> [DOPE *flings the pennies to the left along the ledge.*]

Dope. Get going.

> [ELKUS *and* DOPE *go out right.* BIGGS *and* SKIMMERHORN *come in along the ledge.*]

Biggs. Now it's raining money. I got the price of a morning paper square in the eye.

Skimmerhorn. I've got two thousand five hundred in a breast pocket, five thousand in a side pocket, and five thousand in the billfold.

> [*He slaps his rear.*]

How do I look?

Biggs. No different. Just a lot of slop tied up with string. I've got five thousand in each side pocket and two thousand five hundred in the back. How do I look?

Skimmerhorn. You? All you need now's a pair of wings.

Biggs. Wish I could find the little guy with the big heart that gave us the money. Maybe he'd help us down off this devil's belfry.

Skimmerhorn. How about that shovel? Any possibility of making it pick us up and set us down below there?

Biggs. Well—if anybody was running it, sure. If it swung us over on that dump we could slide the rest of the

way. You might wear out that last five thousand of
yours, the five thousand that's bringing up the rear
there.

Skimmerhorn. When do they come to work in the morning?

Biggs. They won't come to work tomorrow. They can't do
any more till we buy this land.

Skimmerhorn. That's fine. That's just dandy.

Biggs. Nice idea though. Somebody might come along
that could run the engine.

Skimmerhorn. You don't think that boy's coming back
with the sandwiches?

Biggs. No, I don't.

Skimmerhorn. The way I feel inside I may never live to
spend the money.

Biggs. Who you going to leave it to?

Skimmerhorn. Yeah?

Biggs. Oh, all right. Nothing personal.

> [*They sit facing the audience. The* Captain *and* His Crew, *in-
> cluding* DeWitt, *seep in through the rocks about them
> and stand quietly looking on.*]

There was something in that—what you said about
needing a pair of wings.

Skimmerhorn. I should say that wings was the last thing
likely to grow on you. You might grow horns, or a
cloven hoof, or a tail, but wings, no. Not unless somebody slipped up behind you and bashed you over the
head.

Biggs. You know, you'd murder me for what I've got in my pockets?

Skimmerhorn. You thought of it first. Who am I going to leave it to, you said.

Biggs. Just the same I wouldn't feel right if you were standing behind me with a rock in your hand.
[*The* CREW *move in a little.*]

Skimmerhorn. You wouldn't?

Biggs. No. At the moment I wouldn't like to think anybody was creeping up behind me.
[*He stiffens.*]

And by God there is somebody behind me.

Skimmerhorn.
[*Without turning*]

What makes you think so?

Biggs.
[*Running a hand over his hair*]

I just feel it. Turn around, will you? Take a look.

Skimmerhorn.
[*Shivering*]

I will not.—Now you've got me worried.—Or else I'm getting light-headed for lack of food.
[BIGGS *ducks suddenly, as if from an imaginary blow.* SKIMMER-HORN *dodges in sympathy, and with their heads drawn in like turtles they creep forward on hands and knees.*]

Biggs. See anything?

Skimmerhorn. There's nothing there, you ass! What are you dodging? Want to scare me to death? Go on, turn around and face it like a man!

Biggs. Now!

Skimmerhorn. Now!
   [*They whirl in concert, on their knees, facing the* CREW. *They look at each other.*]

Biggs. You're crazy!

Skimmerhorn. I certainly am. And so are you.

Biggs. That isn't there at all. There's nothing there.

Skimmerhorn. All right, you go up and hit it. I'll stay right here, and you go punch it in the nose.
   [BIGGS *stands up.*]

Biggs. Uh—how do you do?—Maybe you—wanted to give us something, huh?
   [*To* DEWITT.]

Uh—I see you brought your friends with you.—If you want the money back you can have it, you know. We don't want the money.
   [*He sticks a hand in his pocket.*]

How much was it now?
   [*The* CREW *look at each other gravely, tapping their foreheads.* SKIMMERHORN *rises.*]

Anything we could do, you know, we'd be glad to do. We're just trying to get down off here.

Skimmerhorn. You know what it is, Art; it's a moving picture company. And have they got the laugh on us?

Thinking they're real. It's all right, boys, we're onto you.

Biggs. Is that so? Say, I guess that's so. Was that moving picture money, you gave us, you fellows? We thought that was real. Ha ha! That's a good one. I guess you must have thought we were pretty funny, backing up that way and jumping around. You had us scared stiff!

[*The* CREW *shake their heads at each other.*]

Skimmerhorn. Come on, now, you aren't bluffing us at all. We've seen the pictures work over at Suffern. We were right out on location there with actors and producers and everything. Some of those girls didn't care whether they wore clothes or not. You're probably used to that where you come from, but I certainly got a kick out of pictures. Fifty chorus girls changing clothes in the bushes over there.

A silence. DEWITT *goes over to the* CAPTAIN *and whispers in his ear.*]

Asher. Lay a hand to it.

[DEWITT *catches hold of the dangling cable.*]

DeWitt. Lay a hand to it, lads. Heave.

[*The* CREW *catch the rope and haul on it, sailor-fashion. The shovel begins to descend.*]

The Crew.

[*Pulling down*]

> Heave! Heave! Heave! Heave!
> Coming a blow, coming a blow;
> Sea runs black; glass runs low;
> Heave! Heave!

Yardarm dips; foam's like snow!
Heave!

[*The shovel touches ground.*]

Biggs. Say, that's an act if I ever saw one. What kind of picture you putting on?

[*The* CAPTAIN *points to the interior of the shovel, looking at* BIGGS *and* SKIMMERHORN.]

What's up, anyway? Want us to go aboard? You know, we were just saying if somebody could run that thing we might get across to the dump and slide down out of here. Think you could swing it across there?

[*The* SAILORS *maneuver behind the two, edging them into the machine.*]

You might haul us up there and not be able to get us down, you know. It's mighty friendly of you to try it, but you'll have your work cut out. Sure, I'll get in. I'll try anything once.

[*He steps in,* SKIMMERHORN *follows reluctantly. The* CAPTAIN *and* DEWITT *guard their retreat. The* SAILORS *catch hold of the cable.*]

Take it easy, now.

The Crew.

Hoist! Hoist! Hoist! Hoist!
Tar on a rope's end, man on a yard.
Wind through an eye-bolt, points on a card;
Hoist! Hoist!
Weevil in the biscuit, rats in the lard,
Hoist!

[*They haul the two up as far as seems necessary, and swing the crane out over the abyss. Then they stop to contemplate their handiwork.*]

Biggs. I'll tell you what—if you catch that line over there some of you can hold back while the rest pull and that'll swing it around.—If that don't work you'd better pull it down again and we'll just wait till morning.

[*The* CREW *continue to stare silently.*]

Skimmerhorn. I'm getting sick at my stomach, boys; you better make it snappy. It gives me the megrims to look down this way.

[*He draws his feet up suddenly.*]

Biggs. Hey, don't rock the boat, you fool! It's a thousand miles straight down!

Skimmerhorn. I'm going to be sick.

Biggs. You better take us down, fellows. It's no good. You can't make it.

DeWitt. How about a game of bowls?

[*The* CAPTAIN *nods.*]

Pieter. Aye, a game of bowls.

[*Led by the* CAPTAIN, *the* CREW *begin to file out.*]

Biggs. Hey, you wouldn't leave us up here, would you? Hey, listen! You! You can have that money back, you know! We don't want the money! What in the name of time?—Listen, what did we ever do to you?—A joke's a joke, after all, but this thing might let go any minute! What's more you're responsible if anything happens to us! There's such a thing as laws in this country!

[*But they have all gone.*]

Skimmerhorn. I'm sick.

Biggs. You'll be sicker before you're out of this mess.— What do you think they meant by that?

Skimmerhorn. I don't know.—Quit kicking me, will you? I'm sick.

Biggs. Well, keep it to yourself.

Skimmerhorn. I wish I thought I could.

Biggs. Help, somebody! Help! We're stuck up here!

Skimmerhorn. What good's that going to do?

Biggs. You don't think they'll leave us here, do you?

Skimmerhorn. I don't know. I don't care. I wish I was dead!—Say, keep away from me, will you? What are you trying to do, pick my pocket?

Biggs. Pick your pocket, you fish? All I ask is keep your feet out of my face.

Skimmerhorn. Well, where in hell's my bill-fold?

Biggs. How do I know? Do you think I took it?

Skimmerhorn. Come on, now. Where is it?
  [*He searches his clothes frantically.*]

Biggs. You're probably sitting on it.—You are sitting on it. There it is.

Skimmerhorn.
  [*Finding it.*]
Jeez, I might have lost it.

Biggs. Now you'd better count it. Just to make sure it's good.

Skimmerhorn. I think I will.
  [*He begins to count the bills.*]

It's good money, Art. Look at it.

Biggs. Not a bad idea, either.

> [*He takes out money and counts it. There is a flash, a long roll and a crash of thunder. Then another and another.*]

Isn't that coming pretty close?

Skimmerhorn. What?

Biggs. The lightning, you fool! Put your money away before you get it wet. You know what I think?

Skimmerhorn. No.

Biggs. There's something up there taking pot shots at us.

Skimmerhorn. There's one thing about money you find. You don't have to pay income tax on it.

Biggs. That's true.

> [*There is a terrific flash, a crash, and the stage is in darkness.*]

That one got the beacon!

> [*Another flash runs right down the crane.*]

Good God, will you quit that? That's close enough!— Say, do you know any prayers?

Skimmerhorn. I know one.

Biggs. Say it, will you?

Skimmerhorn. Matthew, Mark, Luke and John,
Bless the bed that I lie on.

Biggs. That's not much good, that one.

Skimmerhorn. It's the only one I know.—Hey, catch it— hey!

Biggs. What?

[*The lightning is now an almost perpetual illumination, the thunder a constant roll.*]

Skimmerhorn. I dropped fourteen ten dollar bills!

Biggs. Do you know we're going to die here?

Skimmerhorn. We're going to what?

Biggs. Will you quit counting money? We're going to be killed! We're going to die right here in our own steam shovel!

Skimmerhorn. Oh, no. I can't die now. I'm not ready to die!

Biggs. I wish you'd put up your money, then, and pray!

Skimmerhorn. I don't know how to pray.

[*A crash*]

Biggs.

[*On his knees*]

Oh, God, I never did this before, and I don't know how, but keep me safe here and I'll be a better man! I'll put candles on the altar, yes, I'll get that Spring Valley church fixed up, the one that's falling down! I can do a lot for you if you'll let me live! Oh, God—

[*A crash*]

Skimmerhorn.

[*On his knees, his hands full of money*]

Oh, God, you wouldn't do a thing like that, hang us up in our own steam shovel, wet through, and then strike us with lightning! Oh, God, you've been kind to us tonight, and given us things we never expected to get so easy; don't spoil it now!—God damn it, there goes another batch of bills!

[*He snatches at the falling money, and is hauled back by* BIGGS.]

I don't know how to pray! What makes you think there's anybody up there, anyway?

[*Another crash*]

Biggs. Say the one you know then, for God's sake—say it!

Skimmerhorn. Matthew, Mark, Luke and John,
Bless the bed that I lie on!

Biggs. Matthew, Mark, Luke and John,
Bless the bed—Oh, God, I've got an old mother dependent on me; please let me live! Why don't you tell him you'll give the money back?

Skimmerhorn. Because I won't! And you won't, either!

[*A crash*]

Biggs. Now you've done it! Can't you keep anything to yourself? There's such a thing as being politic, even when you're talking to God Almighty!

[*Thunder again*]

CURTAIN

HIGH TOR
ACT TWO

ACT TWO

Scene I

SCENE: *The Tor and the steam shovel as before, only five or six hours later. It's still pitch dark, and* BIGGS *and* SKIMMERHORN *are still in the shovel. They are, however, fast asleep in much the same postures they took formerly on the ground. Under the shovel sits* DEWITT, *picking up and smoothing on his knee a few bills which he has found blowing loose on the rock. The beacon light flashes into the scene.*

DeWitt. There comes on the light again, too, the sweeping light that withers a body's entrails. No sooner out than lit again.—

[Two snores rise from the sleeping pair.]

Aye, take your ease and rest, you detachable Doppelgangers, swollen with lies, protected by the fiends, impervious to lightning, shedding rain like ducks—and why wouldn't you shed rain? your complexions being pure grease and your insides blubber? You can sleep, you can rest. You of the two-bottoms. You make nothing of the lightning playing up and down your backbones, or turning in on cold iron, but a poor sailor out of Holland, what rest has he?—

[He smooths a bill.]

These will be tokens and signs, these will, useful in magic, potent to ward off evil or put a curse on your enemies. Devil's work or not, I shall carry them on me, and make myself a match for these fulminating latter-day spirits.

[He pouches the bills.]

73

I'm hanged if it's not noticeable at once, a sort of Dutch courage infused into the joints and tissues from the mere pocketing up of their infernal numbered papers.

[*He takes out a bill and looks at it.*]

That's sorcery, that's witchcraft, that's black art for you—that's a trick after the old one's heart; why, this stuff would make a man out of a cocked hat and a pair of crutches!

[*He slaps his chest.*]

Now I shall face destiny and take it like a pinch of snuff! Which reminds me I could use a pinch of snuff.

[*He takes out his snuffbox.*]

Snuff? When have I reached for snuff? It would seem to me I haven't gone after snuff in something like two hundred years!

[*He ladles into both nostrils and sneezes violently.*]

Aha, DeWitt! You're a man, DeWitt! A man and a devil! And what shall we wish for now that we have wishing papers in the pockets of our pantaloons? What but a woman, one of these new female furies of theirs, wearing pants like a man, and with nothing to indicate her sex but the general conformation!

[*He draws out bills.*]

Let my woman appear, god of the numbered papers, and let her wear what she likes, so long as a man can make out how she's made. Let her appear within this next three minutes, for God knows how long this mood will last in an old man!

[*He takes another pinch of snuff.*]

Aha! Destiny, present occasions!

[BUDDY *enters carrying beer and sandwiches.*]

Buddy. Hello.

DeWitt. What answer would a man make to that now? That's a strange greeting.

Buddy. Seen a couple of old fat men around anywhere?

DeWitt. Boy, I have seen nothing else all night.

Buddy. Where are they?

DeWitt. You wish to find a couple of old fat men?

Buddy. That's right.

DeWitt. I begin to doubt the supernal powers of these new angel-demons. Here he stands in their presence and asks very foolishly if old DeWitt has seen them.

Buddy. What's foolish about that?

DeWitt. A very cheap, witless little cabin boy unless all signs fail. One who carries packages and lives very badly by the day on half a skilling. A cabin boy.

Buddy. What's the matter with you?

DeWitt. What do you carry in the bag?

Buddy. That's my business.

DeWitt. He has a business then. He is not perhaps so witless as he appears.

Buddy. Are you going to tell me where those two are or do you want me to blow your brains out?

DeWitt. Is my carcass so thin you think to puff my brains out with a breath? Look, 'prentice devil, I am one of you. I bear your signs and symbols. Here you see your own countersign, a cabalistic device of extreme rarity and force. What have you in the bag?

Buddy. Nothing but sandwiches. What do you mean, you're one of us?

DeWitt.

[*Waving a sheaf of bills*]

You should recognize the insignium.

Buddy. Where'd you get it?

DeWitt. It blew away from these same two fat men, 'prentice devil, but now I have it, and it's mine and I obtain power over you. Let me see these sandwiches.

Buddy. It blew away from the fat men, huh? All right, that's what I want to know. It's mine, see? Hand it over.

DeWitt. You reveal yourself a very young and tender 'prentice.

Buddy. Hand it over or I'll fill you full of holes.

[*He sets down his packages and draws a gun, but* DeWitt *is beforehand with two flintlock pistols.*]

DeWitt. You will drop your child's armory on the ground, cabin boy, or I shall pull both triggers at once and blast you halfway to the water.

[Buddy *drops the gun.*]

I tell you I am now a great devil and violent. When I wish merely I have my way.

[Buddy *suddenly takes to his heels.* DeWitt *pulls the triggers one after another; the hammers click but there is no explosion.*]

Why, this new world is not so bad. I am left in posses-
sion of the field.

[*He picks up the automatic and the bag and retreats to his
rock.*]

They fight with the weapons of children. Why, this
new world begins to be mine, to do as I please with.
Whatever kind of witch a sandwich may be come out
and let me interrogate you.

[*He takes out sandwiches.*]

If it be the food eaten by witches and wizards so much
the better, for I am now a wizard myself, and by the
great jib boom I haven't tasted food in God knows
when.

[*He eats.*]

A sweet and excellent morsel, very strong with garlic
and salami, medicinal for the veins and bladder.

[*He looks at his pistols.*]

A little glazed powder in the priming now, and these
two will speak with more authority if it becomes necessary to defend my position.

[*He opens his powder horn and renews the priming.*]

We have seen the time, these blunderbusses and myself,
when we could defend a crow's nest against a whole
crew in mutiny.

[*He pushes away the beer bottles with his foot.*]

I will eat your rations, cabin boy out of the new age,
and I will master you all, men and maids, now that my
strength comes back, but I will not drink your drink.
As Pastor Van Dorf observed very wisely before we
sailed; you may eat the food of the salvages, said he,
when you have voyaged to the new lands overseas; you

may share their rations, you may even make up to their
females after the fashion of sailors when the flesh is
weak, but drink none of their drink, said he, lest it
prove to be Circe's liquor and turn you all to hogs.

[*He eats.*]

Now I have small inclination to be a hog, but a man
I will be, and a very good man, too, of the fieriest
model.

[*He hears* Judith's *step.*]

Take care now, take care! I'm an armed man and a
man of blood!

[Judith *enters.*]

Judith.

[*At some distance*]

I beg your pardon, sir—

DeWitt. A woman, by the great tropical cross, a salvage
woman, come in answer to my unspoken desires.

[*He rises.*]

Your humblest servant, lady salvage; don't run away,
please. I'm a poor lost little man, wouldn't hurt a fly.

Judith. Who are you?

DeWitt. I'm a poor bosun, ma'am, but grown, God knows
how, to something of a person this last quarter hour.

Judith. Are you lost?

DeWitt. Completely adrift, ma'am, on my own mountain.

Judith. I don't think I've seen you before.

DeWitt. That may be, though I'm by way of being one

of the earliest inhabitants, not counting Indians and
Patagonians.

Judith. You live on the mountain?

DeWitt. I maintain a residence here, though the situa-
tion eludes me at the moment.

Judith. Then you are acquainted with Van—Van Dorn?

DeWitt. I have seen him about.

Judith. Have you seen him tonight? I want to find him.

DeWitt. A mere blind, I should say, a maidenly defense,
not to be too forthright; but sent by the talisman she is.

Judith. You have seen him?

DeWitt. God help him, I have, and in none too sancti-
fied an attitude, saving your ladyship, for the lad was
obviously a bit taken with the captain's wife, and she
a married woman of some years' standing, young
though she appear.

Judith. Where was he?
[*She takes a step nearer to him.*]

DeWitt. I was never one to break in on a budding ro-
mance, sweetheart, and out of sheer delicacy I looked
the other way.

Judith. No, but where was he, please? I can show you
the path.

DeWitt. If you hunt out a very pretty little mistress in a
bonnet somewhat behind the fashion, and look under
the bonnet, you may chance to find him there.

Judith. Who are you?

DeWitt. Alpheus DeWitt, your most humble, bosun in the King's navy.

Judith. Forgive me—I shall look elsewhere—

DeWitt. Oh, but I assure you the lad's head over ears, ma'am, and loathe you'd be to interrupt him. Now a pretty lass like yourself should have no trouble replacing one sailor man with another in these stirring times. They come and go like a run of salmon.

Judith. Thank you.

DeWitt. I am myself a notionable lad. Salt tears have been wept for me by one and another.

Judith. No doubt.

DeWitt. I'm a blunt man, but constant and of considerable substance on my own wharf. Could you find it in your heart to love me?

Judith. I'm sorry, no.

DeWitt. To save a sad and desperate man from such a death as the lines of frost on a window? This is a kindly face, this of mine, and a kindly heart under a worn jerkin. These are real tears on my cheeks, too, and I weep them for you, lady.

Judith. I've never seen you till this moment.

DeWitt. Yet you could save me from their sorcery, with one touch of your hand. I waited here for you, and you came.

Judith. You're horrible. Your face is horrible!

DeWitt. Is it, truly?

Judith. Ancient and terrible and horrible!—Tell me where he is. I must know.

DeWitt. I don't know where he is.—You will think better of it. You need only pity me a little at first, or even laugh at me—so you do it kindly—

Judith. I'm in no mood for laughing, though you're ridiculous enough in that get-up.

DeWitt. It's not the latest, I know. And I'm a sad and broken man, lady, lost here among the lesser known peaks on the west side of the world, and looking only for a hand to help me.

Judith. I don't think you're lost at all.

DeWitt. Yes, lady, quite lost.—Nevertheless they run from me! You should have seen the lad run when I snapped my pistols at him.

Judith.

[*Stepping back*]

I should think he would.—Isn't there someone coming there now?

[*She points to the right.* DeWitt *faces about, reaching for his pistols.* Judith *slips away left.*]

DeWitt. If there be, watch what soldierly stand old De-Witt makes in defense of a lady! Come out, children of the new Satan, show yourselves in the light!

[Elkus *and* Dope *appear at right.*]

Elkus. Stick 'em up, bo!

[*They train automatics on him.*]

DeWitt. More toys! Stand back, you cheap new devils!

Elkus. Keep your hands down or I'll let you have it!

DeWitt. Watch now how a man holds off the fiends.
  [*He lifts his pistols.*]

Elkus. Give it to him!
  [*They fire a fusillade at* DeWitt, *who stands unmoved.*]

DeWitt. Firecrackers! You think me a devil like yourselves, to be exorcised with firecrackers?

Elkus. Give it to him again!
  [*They fire once more.*]

DeWitt. Look, you puny devils, I'm a patient man, but
in one moment I shall blow you both into the Tappan
Zee!

Elkus.
  [*Stepping up and pouring bullets into him*]

  Too bad about you!
  [*To* Dope]

  Take the money off him.

Dope. There's something funny about this guy! I can see
right through him!

Elkus. No wonder. He's full of holes as a tennis racket.

Dope. No, by God, I can see through him! Look!
  [*They step back together.*]

Elkus. What kind of a thing are you?

DeWitt. I'm not a man to be daunted by loud noises and
firecrackers, Beelzebub! Go seek your place with the
new father of hell before I send you there! Wizards!

Elkus. Where's the money?

DeWitt. I have a talisman and I ate a sandwich, devils!

Dope. Look, he's a moving picture! He's a regular church window! Look!

DeWitt. Disperse or I fire!

Elkus. Keep out of the way of that sawed-off shotgun!
> [DOPE *suddenly runs in and shoots* DEWITT *through the head, then retreats.*]

DeWitt. I warn you I begin to be annoyed!

Dope. It's no use, chief. I blew his brains out, and he's standing right there!

Biggs.
> [*Looking over the side of the shovel*]

It's a war.

Elkus. Who said that?

Dope. Damned if I know.

Elkus. Beat it.

Dope. Yeah, beat it. Let the money hang. I'm for Canada.

Elkus You said it.
> [*They turn tail. As they are going* DEWITT *fires his pistols in the air.*]

DeWitt. Now am I master of the world of things,
a buccaneer, a devil and a rake!
Women love mastery, and they ran from me;
they ran, these minor devils, ran from DeWitt!
Look where they go there, sweetheart!
> [*He turns.*]

God, she's gone!
Lady! New-world lady! Are you lost?
  [*He follows her.*]

Look now, I've dispersed them, brats and wizards,
spawn out of hell, they ran! I'm master here,
I'm master of the world! Look, lady!
  [*He goes out left.*]

Skimmerhorn. Are you awake?

Biggs. I hope not. I hope this is a nightmare and I wake
up at home in bed.

Skimmerhorn. How did we get here?

Biggs. It must have been something we ate.

Skimmerhorn. I didn't eat anything.

Biggs. There's a bag of sandwiches down there on the
ground.

Skimmerhorn. That's a pleasant thought.

Biggs. Look for yourself.

Skimmerhorn. You're right. It's a bag of sandwiches.

Biggs. Didn't we send somebody for sandwiches and beer,
away back there before all this started?

Skimmerhorn. I don't know. I'm all wet, and I'm stuck
to the shovel.

Biggs. You do seem to be kind of going to pieces. What's
the matter with your toupee?

Skimmerhorn. The glue must have melted.
  [*He takes off his wig.*]

Now I'll catch cold.

Biggs. If any of your constituency sees you in that condition you're out of office for good.

Skimmerhorn. I don't even care if I fall out. I feel terrible.

Biggs. Might be more comfortable for me if you did fall out.
[*He shifts his weight.*]

Skimmerhorn. Sit down! Quit rocking the boat!

Biggs. I've got a cramp. Ouch!

Skimmerhorn. Don't shove me!
[*He pushes* BIGGS.]

Biggs.
[*Pushing back*]

You want to pitch me overboard?

Skimmerhorn. Hey! You know I might have gone out?

Biggs. What do you care?

Skimmerhorn. I'll show you what I care!
[*They lock in a deadly struggle on the verge.*]

Biggs. Wait, Skimmer, look now! If one of us goes down the other goes too. Look at the drop. You don't want to splash on those rocks and I don't either.

Skimmerhorn. Let go then.

Biggs. I'll let go when you do. I'll count three and we'll both let go.

Skimmerhorn. All right.

Biggs. One—two—three.
[*They let go and catch the ropes over the swinging basket.*]

That's better. Now take it easy, buddy. You woke up feeling like poison this morning. After this you count ten when you get an impulse to push anybody.

Skimmerhorn. Same to you.

Biggs. Fine.
[*They sit down cautiously.*]

Skimmerhorn. How in hell did those sandwiches get there?

Biggs. How in hell did we get here?

Skimmerhorn. You haven't got a fishing hook on you, have you?

Biggs. No, I haven't.
[*They sit gloomily looking at the sandwiches.* LISE *and* VAN *come in from the left.*]

Van. Nothing in all the woods
is silent as the owl; you see his shadow
but never hear his wings. The partridge now,
every time he takes off he creaks and cranks
like an old Ford. You never heard such a fuss;
but he's quiet on the ground.

Lise. And is there a squirrel
that flies, bird-fashion?

Van. Well, there's a flying squirrel,
but he's more the glider type. No engine, see,

but he'll do thirty yards. He's on the way
to be a bat if he's not careful.

Lise. How?

Van. He'll leave off tail and put on wing until
he's mostly wing. No doubt the bat was once
some kind of flying mouse.

Lise. Some men have wings.
I've seen them overhead.

Van. That's all put on.
They've no more wings than a goat. When they come
down.

Lise. I've hoped that it was true that men had wings.

Van. Why?

Lise. Oh, they've lived so long, and tried so hard,
and it all comes to nothing.

Van. Having wings,
would that be something?

Lise. Yes, it seems so. And yet
a bird has wings.

Van. And he gets nowhere.

Lise. Yes.
Nothing but just to be a bird, and fly,
and then come down. Always the thing itself
is less than when the seed of it in thought
came to a flower within, but such a flower
as never grows in gardens.

Biggs. Eh—Van Dorn!

Van.

> [*Looking up*]

> What are you doing on the roost, you birds?
> Building a nest?

Biggs. We can't get down.

Van. I'd say
> it ought to be just as easy to get down
> as it was to get up there.

Skimmerhorn. Will you help us out?

Van. You look all right to me. What happened to you?

Biggs. Everything.

Van. How did you get there?

Biggs. God,
> it's a long story.

Van. You've been there all night?

Biggs. Yes, all night.

Van. I wouldn't want to spoil it.
> It's too good to be true. You see those two,
> Lise, there in the scoop?

Lise. They're pitiful.
> Shouldn't you help them?

Van. No. Since time began
> there haven't been two fat-guts that deserved
> a hoisting like those two. In their own machine—
> that makes it perfect.

Lise. What have they done?

Van. They've been
    themselves, that's all. Two thieves, a probate judge
    and a manipulator, hand and glove
    to thieve what they can get. They've got High Tor
    among other things, and mean to carve it down,
    at three cents a square yard.

Lise. These poor old men?

Van. Yes, these poor old men.

Lise. Let them hang there then!

Van. They'll hang there for all me.
    [LISE *and* VAN *turn to go.*]

Skimmerhorn. I'll tell you what,
    Van Dorn, I'll let you have that validation
    if you'll help me down.

Van. That means I'd own the land?

Skimmerhorn. Yes, you'd own it.

Van. Only you'd cancel it,
    once you got down.

Skimmerhorn. To tell the truth I couldn't,
    not if you had the paper.

Van. Toss it over;
    I'd like to see it.
    [SKIMMERHORN *gets out an envelope and throws it to* VAN.]

Biggs. You're a simple judge!
    Now the land's his.

Van. There's a bond goes with this,
    a bond signed by the court. Oh, I looked it up.
    I've read that much law.

Skimmerhorn. Yes, I'll keep the bond
   till we're on your level.

Van. Then I'd advise you both
   to make yourself a nest with two-three sticks,
   like a couple of crows, and settle down to see
   what you can hatch—or maybe lay an egg—
   you'll have plenty of time.

Biggs. Come now, Van Dorn,
   we're in a bad way. It drops off straight down
   a thousand feet here, and Judge Skimmerhorn
   has vertigo. Why, just to save a life,
   out of common humanity, lean on that cable
   and pull us in.

Van. This one?

    [*He pulls. The shovel dips.*]

Biggs. Oh, no, no! God,
   do you want to dump us out!

Van. You said to pull it.

Biggs. Not that one! This! Pull up on that again!
   We're sliding!

Van. Sure.

    [*He rights the shovel.*]

   Now you know how it feels
   when you kick out the props from under men
   and slide 'em on the relief rolls. Ever think
   how that might feel?

Biggs. You don't know what we've both
   been through, Van Dorn. Rained on and struck by
             lightning,

no dinner; we're half-crazy; we've had nightmares,
funny people in hats; that's how we got here,
one of those nightmares!

Van. You sound disconnected.
Maybe you've lost your minds; still I'm not melting
down in my shoes with compunction. The fact is
he's clinging to the bond, Judge Skimmerhorn;
he's not too sunk for that. Now here's my bargain:
You're hanging onto life by one steel cable,
but that's much safer than the spider web
most men have to trust to. Toss me the bond,
Judge Skimmerhorn, or I'll give this line a yank
and you won't even hang.

Skimmerhorn. You wouldn't do it.

Van. Oh, wouldn't I? For a two-cent lollipop
I'd pull the chain right now!

Skimmerhorn. You wouldn't do it!

Van. Hang on, then! Just for a taste, how's the incline
now?
A little steep?
   [*He pulls the line. The shovel tips as before.*]

Biggs. Pull it up! Take the God damn bond!—
throw it to him!

Skimmerhorn. I will not!

Van. Try this then.
   [*He tips the shovel further.*]

Biggs. Give him his bond! I'm slipping!

Skimmerhorn. I will not!

Biggs. I say you will! What good's the money to you
if you're bologny?

Skimmerhorn. What money?

Biggs. You know what money!

Skimmerhorn. Straighten it up.

Van. Do I get the bond?

Skimmerhorn. Hell, yes!
> [VAN *restores their equilibrium.*]

You get the bond if you agree to accept
five thousand for your claim.
> [*He brings out a paper.*]

Van. Don't stall with me!
I'll never have a chance like this again,
and it's hard to resist!

Skimmerhorn. I'm offering you five thousand!
Five thousand! Cash!

Van.
> [*Leaping to the rope.*]

Keep it!

Biggs. Give him his bond!
> [*He wrenches the paper from* SKIMMERHORN *and sails it to* VAN.]

And now you've got it how's five thousand sound?
You settle for it?

Van. Bid against them, Lise. It's a game.
What would you say, Lise?
They offer me five thousand.

Lise. Pieces of silver?

Van. Pieces of silver.

Lise.

    [*Smiling*]

But I'll give you more!
Only five thousand for this crag at dawn
shedding its husk of cloud to face a sunrise
over the silver bay? For silver haze
wrapping the crag at noon, before a storm
cascading silver levin? For winter rains
that run in silver down the black rock's face
under a gray-sedge sky? For loneliness
here on this crag? I offer you nine thousand!
To be paid in silver!

Van. You hear? I've got nine thousand;
  what am I offered?

Biggs. Make it ten thousand—
  and let us down in the bargain!

Van. Yes? Ten thousand?
  A mountain for ten thousand? Hear them, Lise,
  In their despair they lift it by a grand!
  Should it go for ten?

Skimmerhorn. We'll never get it back—
  but that's all right.

Van. Yes, Lise?

Lise. Will they pay
  no more then for the piling of this stone,
  set in its tall hexagonals by fire
  before men were? Searching a hundred kingdoms

men will not find a site for lodge or tower
more kingly! A hundred thousand, sir, in silver,
this is my offer!

Van. Come now, meet it boys—
I have a hundred thousand!

Biggs. She's a fraud!
She's no dealer; she's a ringer, primed
to put the price up! What do you mean by silver?
She won't pay silver!

Van. Coinage of the moon,
but it's current here!

Skimmerhorn. Ten thousand, cash, and that's
the last. Five thousand out of my pocket, see,
and five from Biggs!

  [*He pulls out a bundle of bills.* BIGGS *does the same.*]

Take a good look at cash,
see how that operates!

  [*He tosses down the roll.* BIGGS *follows suit.*]

Van. You go well-heeled
when you go mountain-climbing. Is it real?

Skimmerhorn. Well, look it over. Count it.

  [VAN *takes up one packet, then another.*]

Van. Where did this come from?

Skimmerhorn. Where would you think?

Van. I'll say I got a shock.

  [*He studies the bills again.*]

I don't want your money.

Biggs. What's wrong with it?

Van. Didn't I tell you I had a hundred thousand?
    Take the stuff back. We reckon in moonlight here!
    Put up your mitts!
    [*He tosses the bundles back.*]

Biggs. It's yours if you want it.

Van. No,
    oh, no, I thank you. It's no sale. What's more
    I never meant to sell. The auctioneer's
    about to take a walk.

Biggs. Well, look, we're sitting
    right where we were.

Van. You sit there for your health,
    and think it over.

Skimmerhorn. You won't do that, Van Dorn,
    just leave us here.

Van. Watch me, if you don't think so.
    [*He gives an arm to* LISE.]
    Let me tell you about those babes in the wood,
    did I say they were thieves?
    [*They start out.*]

Biggs. Make it fifteen!

Van. Go to sleep.

Skimmerhorn. Well, twenty! and let us down!

Van. Sweet dreams.

Skimmerhorn. We'll run you out of the state, Van Dorn!

Van. You'll have to get down first!

Skimmerhorn. Is he going away
    and leave us sitting?

Biggs. Looks like it.
    [VAN *and* LISE *move off.*]

Skimmerhorn. Say, Van Dorn,
    will you pitch us up a sandwich?

Van. Sure; they're soggy,
    lying out in the rain.
    [*He returns and tosses sandwiches to them.*]

Biggs. Thanks.

Van. Don't mention it.
    [*He goes out right with* LISE. BIGGS *and* SKIMMERHORN *unwrap*
        sandwiches.]

Skimmerhorn. He got away with that bond.

Biggs. Yeah.

Skimmerhorn. Looks as if we wouldn't make anything on
                    Van Dorn.

Biggs. That's what it looks like.

Skimmerhorn. Christ.

Biggs. Well, we've still got the windfall.

Skimmerhorn. Yeah, we've got that.

Biggs. And here he comes again.

Skimmerhorn. Who?

Biggs. Our mascot, little rabbit's foot, little good-luck
token, little knee-high with the big heart.

> [DeWitt *comes in from the left, looks at the place where the
> sandwiches were and then at the two in the shovel. He
> mutters.*]

DeWitt. Magic again! More devil's work! And the woman
gone, slipped round a turn, and the scent was cold
for an old dog like me. By the mizzen yards,
it's wearing to the temper of a man
even if he's not choleric!—And those two,
those buzzards of evil omen, brooding there
on how they'll cut the mountain like a pie
and sell it off in slices!

> [*He looks at his pistols.*]

One apiece.
It should be just enough, and it's a wonder
I never thought of it.

> [*He lifts his pistols, the two drop their sandwiches into the
> void, and cower down; he clicks the hammers.*]

Damp again! Well, boys,
we'll fix that.

> [*He sits down to freshen the priming.*]

They'll brood over us no more,
those two sea-lions. Damn the rain and mist;
it penetrates the priming! Damn the flint,
and damn the spring! A brace of fine horse-pistols,
that's what the Jew said back in Amsterdam;
it takes a horse to cock 'em. Now then, damn you,
blow 'em off their perch!

> [*As he rises his eye catches something out on the Zee. He stands
> transfixed for a moment, watching.*]

It can't be there!
　　It's there! It's gone! I saw it! Captain Asher!
　　Captain! Captain! Captain! Captain Asher!
　　　　[BIGGS *and* SKIMMERHORN *have ducked down again.* DEWITT
　　　　　rushes out to the right, firing his pistols in the air in his
　　　　　excitement. BIGGS *sits up, then* SKIMMERHORN.]

Skimmerhorn. Am I hurt? Do you see blood anywhere?

Biggs. It seems there was nothing there.
　　　　[*They contemplate the place where* DEWITT *stood.*]

CURTAIN

ACT TWO

SCENE II

SCENE: *Another part of the Tor.* LISE *is sitting high up on a ledge, looking out over the Zee.* VAN *stands near her, looking at her as she speaks. She has his old felt hat in her lap and has woven a wreath of dandelions around the brim. The beacon light strikes athwart her face.*

Lise. But nobody likes this flower?

Van. I like it now.
I used to think it was a weed, but now,
well, it's a flower now.

Lise. The dandelion.
Where will you find another prodigal
so merry or so golden or so wasteful,
pouring out treasure down the sides of hills
and cupping it in valleys?

Van. Buttercups
and touch-me-nots. The touch-me-not's a shoe,
a tiny golden shoe, with a hair-spring latchet
for bees to loosen.

Lise. When did you part from Judith?

Van. Judith?

Lise. When did she go away?

Van. Last evening.
But it seems longer.

Lise. Why?

99

Van. Why, a lot's happened.—
     It's almost morning.

Lise. How do you know?
     [*He steps up to the ledge.*]

Van. See that star,
     that heavy red star back in the west? When that
     goes down, then look for the morning star across
     Long Island Sound, and after that the lights
     dim down in the gray.

Lise. You loved her, very much?

Van. Yes.

Lise. I loved someone too. I love him still.

Van. No, you're mine now.
     [*He sits beside her.*]

Lise. See the great gulf that lies
     between the heavy red star down the west
     and the star that comes with morning? It's a long way.
     There's that much lies between us.

Van. Not for me.

Lise. Even for you.—You're weary?

Van. Well, the truth is
     I sometimes sleep at night.

Lise. Put your head down.
     I'll hold you.
          [*He lays his head on her knees and stretches out.*]

Now I'll wish that I could sing
     and make you sleep. Somehow they're all forgotten,

the old songs. Over and over when the birds
begin at morning I try hard to catch
one tune of theirs. There's one that seems to say:

> Merrily, merrily, chirr, chirr,
> Lueté, lueté, stee—
> Merrily, merrily, chirr, lueté,
> Chirr, lueté, stee.

That's only what it says; for what it sings
you'll have to ask the bird.

Van. I know it, though.
That's the song sparrow.

Lise. Have I come so near?

Van. Say it again.

Lise. I can't. May I ask you something?

Van. Yes.

Lise. There's so much that's changed now men can fly
and hear each other across seas, must men
still die—do they die still?

Van. Oh, yes, they die.
Why do you ask?

Lise. Because I'm still so young,
and yet I can't remember all the years
there must have been.—In a long night sometimes
I try to count them, but they blow in clouds
across the sky, the dancing firefly years,
incredible numbers.—Tell me how old you are
before you go to sleep.

Van. Lying here now
there's not much logic in arithmetic.

Five, or six, maybe. Five or six thousand, maybe.
But when I'm awake I'm twenty-three.

Lise. No more?

Van. No more.

Lise. Tell me why it is I am as I am
and not like you?

Van. I don't know, Lise.

Lise. But tell me.
Have I been enchanted here? I've seen
the trap-rock men, there in the shovel, seeming
so stupid and so pitiful. Could these
use charms and rites to hold wrecked mariners
forever in a deep cataleptic spell
high on a mountain-fringe?

Van. The trap-rock men?
They're no more wizards than I am. They buy
and sell, and when they've had their fill of dust
they die like the rest of us.

Lise. But they laid spells
about us?

Van. There are no wizards and no spells.
Just men and women and money and the earth
the way it always was. The trap-rock men
don't know you're here.

Lise. It's not sorcery then. If I had died
and left my bones here on the mountain-top
but had no memory of it, and lived on
in dreams, it might be as it is. As children

sure we were told of living after death,
but there were angels there, and onyx stone
paving an angel city, and they sang
eternally, no darkness and no sun,
nothing of earth. Now can it be men die
and carry thence no memory of death,
only this curious lightness of the hands,
only this curious darkness of the mind,
only to be still changeless with the winters
passing; not gray, not lined, not stricken down,
but stamped forever on the moving air,
an echo and an image? Restless still
with the old hungers, drifting among men,
till one by one forgotten, fading out
like an old writing, undecipherable,
we lose our hold and go? Could it be true?
Could this be how men die?

Van.

    [*Half asleep*]

It may be, Lise.
I love you when you speak.

Lise. And I love you.
But I am dead, and all the crew is dead;
all of the *Onrust* crew—and we have clung
beyond our place and time, on into a world
unreal as sleep, unreal as this your sleep
that comes upon you now. Oh, you were cruel
to love me and to tell me I am dead
and lie here warm and living! When you wake
we shall be parted—you will have a world
but I'll have none! There's a chill falls on me,
the night-dew gathering, or my mind's death chill—

knowing at last I know.—You haven't heard.
You told me this in a half-dream. You've been kind.
You never thought to hurt me. Are you asleep?

Van. I think I was.

Lise. Sleep, sleep. There was once a song,
if only I could call back air and words,
about a king who watched a goblet rising
and falling in the sea. It came to land
and on the rim the king's name was inscribed
with a date many years before. Oh, many years,
a hundred or three hundred. Then he knew
that all his life was lived in an old time,
swept out, given to the waters. What remained
was but this goblet swimming in the sea,
touching his dust by chance.—But he's asleep.
And very well he might be with dull stories
out of old songs.—Sleep, sweet; let me have
your head here on my knees, only this night,
and your brown hair round my finger.

> [*A girl's shadowy figure comes in from the right, walking lightly, pauses, as if at seeing them, and turns to go, the face still unrevealed.*]

Are you Judith?

Judith. Yes.

Lise. The lad's asleep, but when he wakes
you'll have him back.

Judith. Do you dispose of him
just as you please?

Lise. No. It's not what I please.
It's what will happen.

Judith. I don't know who you are.

Lise. I'm but a friend of his. You left him bitter
 going away so lightly. I was bitter—
 and so we tried to play at being lovers,
 but it won't do. He'll wake, and he'll be yours,
 all as it was. Only if I may hold him
 while he lies here asleep, it helps a little
 and I'll be happier.

Judith. You'll keep him then
 after he wakes.

Lise. No.

Judith. Then why are you crying?

Lise. Am I crying?
 Well, they're not for him, nor you, these tears;
 something so far away, so long ago,
 so hopeless, so fallen, so lost, so deep in dust
 the names wash from the urns, summons my tears,
 not love or longing. Only when you have him,
 love him a little better for your sake,
 for your sake only, knowing how bitterly
 I cried, for times past and things done.

Judith. You're strange—
 the dress you wear's strange, too.—Who are you then?
 I'm—afraid of you!

Lise. Afraid of tears
 and a voice out of long ago? It's all I have.

Judith. No—no—I'm not afraid. Only for him.
 I've done my crying, too.—Shall I come back?

Lise. Don't wake him now. Come back at dawn. You'll
                          find him
    here alone.

> [Two *or* Three Sailors *appear on the rocks at the rear, looking
> out over the Zee.*]

Pieter. Look for yourself.

A Sailor. Aye.

Pieter. Do you make her out?

The Sailor. She's the square top-yards.

Another Sailor. Now, God, if it were she!

Pieter. It's the brigantine! The *Onrust* from up-river
    tacking this way!

Asher.

> [*Outside*]

    Lise! Lise! Lise!

> [*The* Captain *comes in at the rear with* DeWitt.]

    Lise, the ship's on the river! Quick, there's haste!
    She must catch the tide down-stream!

Lise. Hush! Hush! You'll wake him!

Asher. But look across the Zee! The *Onrust's* in
    and waiting for us!

Lise. But you say it, Asher,
    only to comfort me. There is no ship,
    nor are we caught in spells here, or enchanted,
    but spectres of an old time. The life we live
    is but a lingering, a clinging on,

our dust remembering. There is no ship,
only a phantom haunting down the Zee
as we still haunt the heights.

Asher. Look! The *Onrust!*
Look, Lise!

Lise. Yes, I see it.

Asher. Will you come?

Lise. Why would I stay? Why would I go? For go
or stay we're phantoms still.

Asher. But will you come?
Who is this lad?

Lise. Her lad. But he was hurt
and fell asleep.
[VAN *wakes and lifts his head.*]

Asher. Come quickly!

Lise. Yes, for his sake
it's better I should go.

Van. Where must you go?
[*She rises.*]

Lise. The *Onrust's* on the river
and we must catch the tide.

Van. Would you leave me now?

Lise. Yes, I must leave you.

Van. You'll go back with him?

Lise. Yes.

Van. And was nothing meant of all we said?

Lise. What could we mean, we two? Your hurt's quite
                              cured
and mine's past curing.

Van. Let me go with you then.

Lise. I should have told you if I'd only known
how we stood at the tangent of two worlds
that touched an instant like two wings of storm
drawn out of night; touched and flew off, and, falling,
fall now asunder through a wide abyss,
not to touch again.

   [*She steps back among the rocks.*]

Van. Let them go if they like!
What do I care about worlds? Any world you have
I'll make it mine!

Lise. You told me in your sleep.
There is no witchcraft. Men are as they were;
we're parted now.

Van. Give me your hand again!
   They dare not take you from me, dare not touch you
no matter who they are, or where they come from—
they have no hold on us!

Lise. If I could stay!
If I could stay with you. And tend my garden
only a little longer!

Van. Put out your hand!

Lise. There were too many, many, many years.

Van. I'll be alone here—

Lise. No, not alone. When you must walk the air,
    as all must walk it sometime, with a tread
    that stirs no leaf, and breathe here with a breath
    that blows impalpable through smoke or cloud,
    when you are as I am, a bending wind
    along the grain, think of me sometimes then
    and how I clung to earth. The earth you have
    seems now so hard and firm, with all its colors
    sharp for the eye, as a taste's sharp to the tongue,
    you'll hardly credit how its outlines blur
    and wear out as you wear. Play now with fire
    while fire will burn, bend down the bough and eat
    before the fruit falls. For there comes a time
    when the great sun-lit pattern of the earth
    shakes like an image under water, darkens,
    dims, and the clearest voices that we knew
    are sunken bells, dead sullen under sea,
    receding. Look in her eyes.
       [VAN *looks at* JUDITH.]

Asher. Come!

Lise. See, the dawn
    points with one purple finger at a star
    to put it out. When it has quite gone out
    then we'll be gone.
       [VAN *looks at the dawn, then turns back toward* LISE.]

Van. Lise! Lise!
       [*But even as he speaks* LISE *and the* CREW *have disappeared.*]

Lise.

       [*Unseen*]

    This is your age, your dawn, your life to live.
    The morning light strikes through us, and the wind

that follows after rain tugs at our sails—
and so we go.

DeWitt.

   [*Still half-seen*]

And welcome you are to the age, too, an age of witches
and sandwiches, an age of paper, an age of paper money
and paper men, so that a poor Dutch wraith's more
                                              man
than the thickest of you!

   [*He steps back and vanishes. It is now dawn.*]

Van. She never said good-bye.

Judith. There is a ship.

Van. Yes?

Judith. Tiny, with black, square sails;
   low and small.

Van.

   [*Still looking after* Lise]

She'll be a phantom too
like all the rest. The canvas casts no shadow;
the light sifts through the spars. A moonlight rig
no doubt they call it.

Judith. I think I hear their voices
   as they go down the crag.

Van. But you won't see them.
   No matter what you hear.

The Sailors.

   [*A wisp of chantey in the distance*]

Coming a blow, coming a blow,
sea runs black, glass runs low.

Van. Just voices down the wind.
Why, then they were all mist, a fog that hangs
along the crevices of hills, a kind
of memory of things you read in books,
things you thought you'd forgotten. She was here,
and she was real, but she was cloud, and gone,
and the hill's barren of her.

Judith. There are no ghosts.

Van. I know—but these were ghosts or I'm a ghost,
and all of us. God knows where we leave off
and ghosts begin. God knows where ghosts leave off
and we begin.

Judith. You were in love with her.

Van. She leaves the mountain barren now she's gone.
And she was beautiful.

Judith. I came to tell you
that I was wrong—I mean about the land—
what you have here is better than one buys
down in the towns. But since I come too late
I'll say it and then go.—Your way was best.
I think it always would be.—So, good night, Van—
or, rather, it's good morning.

Van. Yes, it's morning.—
Is it too late?

Judith. Oh, Van, I think it is.
It was for Lise you were calling, not
for Judith. I can't say I blame you much,

because she is more beautiful. And yet
you love her, and not me. You'll say they're ghosts
and won't come back. Perhaps. I'm not so certain
about the way of ghosts. She may come back.
And you still love her.

Van. There's no ship at all.
It faded in the dawn. And all the mists
that hung about the Tor, look how they lift,
pouring downstream with the wind. Whatever it was,
was said, or came between us, it's all gone
now it's daylight again.

Judith. I came to say
if only I could keep you, you should keep
the Tor, or what you wished. I'm sorry I went.
I'm sorry this has happened. But it has.
And so—

Van. Should I keep the Tor?

Judith. Yes, if you like.

Van. God knows they haven't left me much of it.
Look, where the new road winds along the ledge.
Look at the jagged cut the quarries make
down to the south, and there's a boy scout trail
running along the ridge Mount Ivy way,
where they try out their hatchets. There's the light,
and steps cut into stone the linesmen blew
for better climbing. The crusher underneath
dumps road rock into barges all day long
and sometimes half the night. The West Shore tunnel
belches its trains above the dead lagoons
that line the brickyards. Their damned shovel hangs

across my line, ready to gouge the peak
we're standing on. Maybe I'm ghost myself
trying to hold an age back with my hands;
maybe we're all the same, these ghosts of Dutchmen
and one poor superannuated Indian
and one last hunter, clinging to his land
because he's always had it. Like a wasp
that tries to build a nest above your door—
and when you brush it down he builds again,
then when you brush it down he builds again—
but after a while you get him.

Judith. Then you'll sell?

Van. I guess if you were with me then we'd sell
for what we could, and move out farther west
where a man's land's his own. But if I'm here
alone, I'll play the solitary wasp
and sting them till they get me.

Judith. If it's your way
then it's your way.

Van. I'll sell it if you'll stay.
Won't you stay with me, Judith?

Judith. I think I'd always hear you calling Lise
while I was standing by. I took a wrong turning
once, when I left you and went down the hill,
and now it may not ever be the same.
  [*She turns.*]

CURTAIN

HIGH TOR

ACT THREE

ACT THREE

SCENE: *The shovel still hangs over the verge, and* BIGGS *and* SKIM-
MERHORN *still occupy it. The rising sun sends level rays across
the rock, lighting their intent faces as they stare downward.*
BIGGS *has torn a handkerchief into strips and tied them together
into a string. He appears to be fishing for something which lies
below the ledge, out of view of the audience. Over and over
he tries his cast.*

Skimmerhorn. Little to the left.

Biggs. You don't say?

Skimmerhorn. Little to the right.

Biggs. Put it to a tune and sing it, why don't you?

Skimmerhorn. There! Almost!

Biggs. I don't need any umpire.

Skimmerhorn. Let me try it.

Biggs. Oh, no. You always were a butter-fingers.
   [*The string tightens.*]

   By Golly!

Skimmerhorn. It's on!

Biggs. You're explaining to me?
   [*He pulls up. A bottle of beer emerges from below.*]

Skimmerhorn. Fifty per cent!

Biggs. What?
   [*He pauses, the bottle in air.*]

117

Skimmerhorn. You tore up my handkerchief! Fifty per
cent. That's the natural division between capital and
labor.

Biggs. Oh, now I'm labor and you're capital.
   [*He pulls up carefully.*]

Skimmerhorn. Fifty per cent!

Biggs. I get the first pull at it. That's all I ask.
   [*The string parts, and the bottle descends silently into the void.*]
That's that.

Skimmerhorn. You should 'a let me handle it.

Biggs. Yeah. No doubt.

Skimmerhorn. Am I thirsty?

Biggs. Wait till the sun gets up a little. We'll be pan-fried
in this thing.

Skimmerhorn. Look!
   [*He points down the rocks.*]

Biggs. If it's more of those little people I give up.

Skimmerhorn. It's a trooper.

Biggs. What do you know? Up early for a trooper, too.
Listen, about that stuff in our pockets?

Skimmerhorn. Yeah?

Biggs. Do we say anything about it?

Skimmerhorn. Do you?

Biggs. Do you?

Skimmerhorn. No.

Biggs. Neither do I, then.

Skimmerhorn. Beautiful morning.

Biggs. I always say it's worth while being up early just to catch the sunrise.

[*A* TROOPER *climbs in followed by* SKIMMERHORN SENIOR.)

The Trooper. Hello!

Biggs. Hello, Patsy.

Patsy. Say, you boys had the wives worried down in Ledentown. Been looking for you all night. There they are, Mr. Skimmerhorn.

Skimmerhorn, Sr.
[*Winded*]

Good God!
[*He sits, a hand to his heart.*]

And I climbed up here. We thought you were under that rock slide.

Skimmerhorn. I guess you're disappointed.

Senior. The next time you two go on a bat and spend a night up a tree you can stay there and sober up.

Skimmerhorn. We haven't been drinking.

Senior.
[*Pointing to a bottle*]

What's that?

Skimmerhorn. Beer. But we didn't have a drop to drink. I'd certainly appreciate a swallow of that now.

Patsy.
[*Tossing up bottle*]

Here you are. Hair of the dog that bit you.

Biggs. We're not drunk. We're dry. We didn't have a drop to drink nor a bite to eat.

Patsy. All right. All right. Only the ground's covered with beer and sandwiches.

Biggs. You tell 'em how it was, Skimmer.

Skimmerhorn. You tell 'em.

Biggs. Well, you see, the whole thing's pretty complicated.

Patsy. I know. I've been through it. You wake up in the morning and you can't believe it yourself.

Biggs. I don't mean that. I'm sober as a judge.

Patsy. Yeah, what judge?
[*He hauls at a cable.*]

Can you lend me a hand with this, A.B.?

Senior. Give me a minute.
[*The shovel tips.*]

Biggs. Hey, not that one! The other one!

Patsy. Sorry. Not much of a mechanic.

Biggs. Straighten it up again.
[*Patsy does so.*]

Skimmerhorn. Are we never getting off this? My legs are paralyzed sitting here.

Biggs. So are mine.

Patsy.

[*Hauling down*]

It's too much for me alone.

Skimmerhorn. Got your wind yet, A.B.?

Senior. I don't know whether I want you down yet. You had your good time, now you can put in a few minutes paying for it.

Skimmerhorn. Oh, we had a good time, did we?

Senior. What were you doing? You came up here to buy Van Dorn's property; you're gone all night, and the whole damn town's up all night hunting for you! And we find you up in a steam shovel enjoying a hang-over!

Patsy. And now I know what a hang-over looks like.

Biggs. I tell you we didn't even have a drink of water!

Senior. I believe that!

Biggs. And we're thirsty! Have you got an opener?

Patsy. No, I haven't.

Senior. Before you open anything tell me what you were doing last night. Did you see Van Dorn?

Skimmerhorn. Sure we saw him.

Senior. Well, what did he say?

Skimmerhorn. He said no.

Senior. And I suppose that took all night?

Skimmerhorn. We had an argument.

Senior. And then he chased you up the crane, I suppose?

Skimmerhorn. No.

Senior. Well, how did you get up there?

Skimmerhorn. We were hauled up.

Senior. All right. Who hauled you up?

Skimmerhorn. You tell him, Art.

Biggs. Oh, no. You tell him.

Skimmerhorn. As a matter of fact, I don't think it happened.

Senior. You're there, aren't you?

Skimmerhorn. Yes, we're here.

Senior. Well, if you weren't drunk how did you get there?

Skimmerhorn. Well, you see, first we tried to negotiate with Van Dorn.

Senior. And he wouldn't take the money?

Skimmerhorn. That's right.

Senior. Did you tell him he didn't really own the land? Till the will was validated?

Skimmerhorn. Yes, we told him that.

Senior. And he still wouldn't talk business?

Skimmerhorn. He's stubborn. Stubborn as a mule.

Senior. Did you tell him you could take the land away from him?

Skimmerhorn. Oh, yes.

Senior. And you offered him the twenty-five thousand?

Biggs. We offered him a fair price.

Senior. You were authorized to say twenty-five thousand.

Biggs. We didn't quite get to that. We offered ten.

Skimmerhorn. You see, we thought we'd save the company some money.

Senior. I'll bet you did. You thought you'd make a little on the side, and I'd never know.

Skimmerhorn. Oh, no.

Biggs. Oh, no.

Senior. All right, you offered ten and he wouldn't take it. Then what happened?

Skimmerhorn. Well, we couldn't get down because of the slide, so some sailors offered to let us down in this thing.

Senior. Sailors—up here?

Skimmerhorn. Little men, in big hats.

Biggs. Might have been a moving picture company.

Senior. Yeah? Any elephants? Or snakes?

Skimmerhorn. We're trying to tell you the truth!

Patsy. Certainly sounds like delirium tremens, boys.

Senior. Never mind, you were hauled up by pink elephants, and then what?

Skimmerhorn. Van Dorn came along and started to dump us down the cliff.

Senior. What's Van Dorn look like? Kind of an octopus, with long feelers?

Skimmerhorn. Are you going to let us down out of this basket?

Senior. No. Not till you come across with what's been going on.

Skimmerhorn. All right. I'll talk when I'm down.

Senior. Can a grown man get pie-eyed on beer?

Patsy. Must have been something stronger.
[VAN DORN *comes in from the right.*]

Senior. Who are you?

Van. Oh, I'm nobody. I just own the property.

Senior. What property?

Van. This.

Senior. Are you Van Dorn?

Van. I am.

Senior. I'm A. B. Skimmerhorn, Mr. Van Dorn, president of Igneous Trap-rock, and I'm glad to meet you.
[*He puts out a hand.*]

Van.
[*Ignoring the hand*]
Are these friends of yours?

Senior. One's a nephew and one's a partner. Why?

Van. Because any friend of theirs is no friend of mine.

[JUDITH *and* THE INDIAN *enter at the rear. She is leading him.*]

Patsy. Who do you think you're talking to?

Van. A. B. Skimmerhorn, of Skimmerhorn, Skimmerhorn, Biggs and Skimmerhorn, small-time crooks and petty thieving done. Cheap.

Senior. Now, to be frank, there may have been some misunderstanding, Mr. Van Dorn. Those two were hardly in condition to negotiate. But I can offer you a fair price for your land, and if you don't take it we may have to push you a little, because we want this acreage and we intend to have it.

Skimmerhorn. He's got the validation papers.

Senior. You gave him the validation papers?

Biggs. We had to. He started to trip the machine.

Senior. That puts us in a sweet mess, that does. Will you take twenty-five thousand?

Van. No.

Senior. Will you take fifty thousand?

Van. No.

Senior. Then we go home, and the machinery can rust here. That's the best I can do.

Van. Fine. Let it rust.

Judith. Van?

Van. Yes, Judith.

Judith. There's someone here to see you.

Van. You want to see me, John?

The Indian. But I can wait. I have time enough.

Van. I'll be right with you.

Judith. I had to bring him, Van, because he said
   his eyes were bad. He couldn't see the way.

Van. Thanks, Judith.

Senior. Look, Van Dorn, you know the saying,
   every man has his price. I've heard it said
   God has his price, if you'll go high enough.
   Set a figure.

Van. I'm not thinking of prices.
   I don't want to sell. Hell, fifty thousand's
   too much money for me.

Senior. We'll give you less.

Van. I don't want less or more. It's not a matter
   of money.

Senior. Will you take a partnership
   in the company?

Van. No.

Senior. Good God, what do you want?

Van. I want to have it back the way it was
   before you came here. And I won't get that. I know
   what kind of fool I look to all of you,
   all but old John there. But I'll be a fool
   along with John, and keep my own, before

I let you have an inch. John, fifty thousand
or this old hill-top. Is it worth keeping?

The Indian. **No.**

Van. No?

The Indian. It's gone already. Not worth keeping.

Van. I thought you'd say it was. I counted on you
   to be my friend in that.

The Indian. It's an old question,
   one I heard often talked of round the fire
   when the hills and I were younger. Then as now
   the young braves were for keeping what was ours
   whatever it cost in blood. And they did try,
   but when they'd paid their blood, and still must sell,
   the price was always less than what it was
   before their blood was paid.

Van. Well, that may be.

The Indian. I wish now I had listened when they spoke
   their prophecies, the sachems of the tents;
   they were wiser than I knew. Wisest of all,
   Iachim, had his camp here on this Tor
   before the railroad came. I saw him stand
   and look out toward the west, toward the sun dying,
   and say, "Our god is now the setting sun,
   and we must follow it. For other races,
   out of the east, will live here in their time,
   one following another. Each will build
   its cities, and its monuments to gods
   we dare not worship. Some will come with ships,
   and some with wings, and each will desecrate

the altars of the people overthrown,
but none will live forever. Each will live
its little time, and fly before the feet
of those who follow after." Let them come in
despoiling, for a time is but a time
and these will not endure. This little hill,
let them have the little hill, and find your peace
beyond, for there's no hill worth a man's peace
while he may live and find it. But they fought it out
and died, and sleep here.

Senior. Why, this is a wise Indian.
A little pessimistic about the aims
of civilization, but wise anyway.
What do you say, Van Dorn?

The Indian. You too will go
like gnats on the wind. An evening and a day,
but still you have your day. Build monuments
and worship at your temples. But you too
will go.

Senior. You're on my side, so I don't mind,
but you have a damned uncomfortable way
of speaking. I'm a Republican myself,
but I don't go that far! What do you say, Van Dorn?
Can we do business?

Van. Judith?

Judith. I'm out of it.
It's your decision. I'd say keep it though
if you want to keep it.

Van. I'll sell it. Fifty thousand.
On one condition. There's a burying ground
I want to keep.

Senior. Sure. That can be arranged.
It's settled, then. Come down to Ledentown
tomorrow and get your money.

Van. Yes, I'll come.

Senior. Why three cheers, boys. We're out of the woods.
Take hold,
Van Dorn, and swing these topers off the limb.
Then they can sign the pledge.
[*A* TROOPER *appears with* ELKUS *and* DOPE.]

Budge (The Trooper). Help me keep an eye on these two, will you, Patsy? I've got a confession out of them on the Nanuet bank robbery, and they say the money's up here.

Patsy. Up here? Whereabouts?

Budge. They left it in a satchel.

Patsy. There's the satchel, all right.
[*He examines it.*]
Empty.

Budge. Looks like a stall, you guys. You buried it.

Elkus. Didn't keep a cent, officer. Somebody up here got it.

Budge. Well, who?

Elkus. Last time I saw it one of those birds sat down on it.
[*He points to* BIGGS *and* SKIMMERHORN.]

Patsy. You know who they are? That's Judge Skimmer-horn of the Probate Court, and Arthur Biggs of the Trap-rock Company.

Elkus. Well, one of them sat down on it.

Budge. Why didn't he pick it up?

Elkus. I don't know whether he saw it.

Dope. And then there was a little guy in a big hat that had some of it.

Patsy. Yeah? Who?

Budge. That's right. Buddy said something about a little guy in a big hat.

Patsy. You think he got away with it?

Elkus. He had some of it, and we haven't got a cent.

Budge. So now we have to look for a little guy in a big hat. Any other description?

Elkus. Short and fat, had two sawed-off shotguns, and wore knee-pants.

Dope. And you could see right through him.

    [BUDGE *is writing in a notebook.*]

Patsy. What?

Dope. You could see right through him.

Budge. I'm beginning to think I can see right through you.

Patsy. Check on that. Elkus, you saw him. Could you see through him?

Elkus. Certainly was a funny-looking guy. Looked as if you could see right through him.

Budge. You expect me to send that out over the country: "Look for a short, fat man with a big hat and two sawed-off shotguns. Dangerous. You can see right through him."?

Patsy. They buried the money, Budge. Or else they're screwy.

Elkus. I thought I was screwy. You couldn't hurt him with a gun.

Budge. What do you mean?

Dope. We bored him full of holes and he wouldn't even sit down.

Budge. You mean he kept on running?

Dope. Running? He just stood there and let us shoot him. Like shooting through a window.

Budge. Must have been wearing a vest.

Dope. I shot him through the head! Two feet away! And it just made him mad!

Patsy. Take 'em away, Budge. They're nuts.

Elkus. But he had the money! Buddy saw him with the money!

Patsy. They're all three nuts.

Budge. I never heard a line like that before.

Patsy. Who lives around here?

Van. I guess I'm the only one that lives near-by.

Patsy. Did you hear any shooting last night?

Van. Plenty of it.

Patsy. Did you take a look round?

Van. Yes, I did.

Patsy. Did you see a little guy in a big hat?

Van. Six or seven of them.

Budge. What!

Van. Six or seven of them.

Budge. I suppose you could see right through them?

Van. Once in a while.

Budge. I'm going to quit writing this down. There's enough here to get me fired already.

Patsy. If you saw six or seven where did they go?

Van. Down the river.

Patsy. In a car?

Van. In a ship.

Patsy. Sounds like a motor-boat gang. Well, that's something. They went down the river.

Van. But I can tell you where there's thirty dollars of the money.

Budge. Where?

Van. On the ledge there below the shovel.
    [BUDGE *and* PATSY *step over to look.*]

Budge. There it is. Three ten dollar bills. How did it get there?

Van. I don't know. I just happened to see it.

Budge. Did you try to get it?

Van. No. I thought it probably belonged to the gentlemen up there in the scoop.

Patsy. Did one of you drop some money, Judge?

Skimmerhorn. I don't think so. Not me.

Biggs. Not me.

Patsy. Did either of you see a little man in a big hat?
[*The two look at each other.*]

Skimmerhorn. Why, yes, we did.
[PATSY *and* BUDGE *look at each other.*]

Budge. Well, if they say so he must have been here.

Patsy. What was he doing?

Skimmerhorn. He was fighting with those two.
[*He points to* ELKUS *and* DOPE.]

Biggs. A regular war.

Patsy. Say, listen to that.

Budge. Do you know if he took anything out of the
satchel?

Skimmerhorn. Yes, I think he did. He had the satchel.

Budge. Now we're getting somewhere.

Patsy. You don't know where he went?

Skimmerhorn. No.

Patsy. If you saw anything else that might give us a clue—?

Skimmerhorn. No, not a thing.

Patsy. It beats me.

Van. Want me to suggest a question?

Patsy. What?

Van. Ask the Judge if he gained any weight during the night.

Patsy. What's the matter with you?

Van. Looks to me like he picked up a good deal.

Patsy. I'll think up my own questions, thanks. Might as well trundle the yeggs back to jail, Budge. Whoever got the stuff it's gone.

Budge. That's what it looks like.

Van. Aren't you going to help the Judge down before you go?

Biggs. Oh, don't bother. We'll get down.

Skimmerhorn. No hurry. We're all right. You take care of your prisoners.

Patsy. Might as well lend a hand while we're here.

Biggs. Run along, boys. We're all right. Don't worry about us.

Patsy.

[*To* Budge]

Want to wait a minute?

Budge. Well, I'm due back, if they can make it themselves.

Biggs. Sure.

Van. Oh, don't leave those poor fellows up on that crane! They've been there all night!

Skimmerhorn. We're fine. You run along.

Budge. Well, take a drag on the rope, Patsy. I'll wait.
> [PATSY *and* VAN *haul the shovel down.*]

Skimmerhorn. No need to go to all this trouble.

Patsy. No trouble at all.

Van. A pleasure. Why you were asking me all night to get you out of this.
> [*The shovel touches ground. The two sit still.*]

Patsy. What's the matter?

Skimmerhorn. Guess my legs are asleep.

Biggs. Mine too.

Patsy. I'll help you up.
> [*They are pulled to their feet, staggering. Their pockets are very obvious.*]

Budge. How about it? O.K.?

Patsy. All set. Say, you are loaded down. Carried plenty of lunch, I guess?

Biggs. Oh, we brought plenty.

Van.
> [*Tapping* BIGGS' *pocket*]

I told you they gained weight. Something in the air up here.

Elkus. Couldn't be money, could it?

Biggs. As a matter of fact, some of it is. We were carrying cash to pay Van Dorn for his farm.

Patsy. Cash?

Biggs. Yeah, cash.

Patsy. How much?

Biggs. Just what we were authorized to pay. Twenty-five thousand.

Van. Funny thing, too. It's got the Orangeburg pay roll stamp on it.

Biggs. Well, hardly.

Patsy. What makes you think so?

Van. I saw it. They offered me ten thousand.

Patsy. Just for the record, I'd better look at it, Judge.

Skimmerhorn. I wouldn't if I were you. I'm hardly under suspicion of bank robbery.

Patsy. I'll take a look at it.
  [*He holds out a hand.* BIGGS *passes him a package.*]

Senior. I don't get this at all.

Patsy. It's got the Orangeburg stamp on it, all right.

Skimmerhorn. Must be some mistake. They must have got the money mixed at the bank.

Patsy. Sure. Well, if that's all we can easy check on that.

Van. Sure. You'd better check on it.

Skimmerhorn. Are you under the impression that we robbed the bank?

Van. You explain it. I can't.

Senior. You say you drew the money to pay Van Dorn?

Skimmerhorn. That's right, A.B.

Senior. And it's got the Orangeburg label on it?

Skimmerhorn. That's what they say.

Senior. I'll have something to say to the bank about that.

Skimmerhorn. Oh, I'll take care of it. Just a clerical error.

Patsy. I'm afraid I'll have to take the money, though. Oh, you'll get your own money back, but if this is the Orangeburg money—

Biggs. Sure, take it.
  [*They unload.*]

Patsy. And I guess I really ought to put you both under arrest.

Biggs. What? Under arrest?

Patsy. Wouldn't you say so, Budge?

Budge. Don't see any way out of it. Doesn't mean anything. Just an examination.

Skimmerhorn. I'd like to keep it out of the papers, if possible, of course. An examination might be very embarrassing—you see, I have political enemies.

Biggs. Always ready to think the worst of a man, and print it, too.

Patsy. Still, I guess we'll have to have an examination. Just for the record.

Skimmerhorn. You know who we are, of course?

Patsy. Yes, sir.

Skimmerhorn. I won't submit to an examination! It's preposterous!

Patsy. I don't see how we can get out of it, though. Because we had a robbery, and here's the money, and we've got to explain it somehow.

Skimmerhorn. I won't submit to it!

Patsy. You got an extra pair of handcuffs there, Budge?

Budge. Yeah.

Skimmerhorn. All right. I'll go.

Biggs. Sure. We'll go. And we'll make a lot of people sorry!

Patsy. Go on ahead, Budge.

 [BUDGE *starts out with his prisoners.*]

Dope. But how about the little guy with the big hat? How about him?

Budge. I'll tell you about him. It's entirely possible there wasn't any little guy in a big hat.

Dope. But we all saw him!

Budge. Oh, no, you didn't see him. You saw right through him. And the reason was he wasn't there.

 [BUDGE, ELKUS *and* DOPE *go out.*]

Biggs. You don't think we made that up, about the man in the big hat?

Patsy. Well, you have to admit it doesn't sound exactly plausible.

[PATSY, BIGGS *and* SKIMMERHORN *go out.*]

Senior.

[*As he goes*]

It shakes a man's faith in evidence.

[*To* VAN]

See you tomorrow.

Van. I'll be there.

[SKIMMERHORN SENIOR *goes out.*]

So now—I've sold the Tor.

The Indian. Yes, but it's better.

Van. Better than living on a grudge, I guess.
It might come down to that.

The Indian. There's wilder land,
and there are higher mountains, in the west.

Van. Out Port Jervis way.

The Indian. Perhaps. You'll find them.

Judith. He came to tell you, Van—this is his death-day.
I'll go now.

Van. All right, John.

The Indian. Could I keep it?
The hand I held? It's a new thing, being blind,
when you've had an Indian's eyes.

[JUDITH *returns and gives him her hand again.*]

Judith. I'll stay a while.

The Indian. When I had lost the path
   halfway along the ridge, there at my feet
   I heard a woman crying. We came on
   together, for she led me. There'll be time
   for crying later. Take her west with you.
   She'll forget the mountain.

Van. Will you come?

Judith. I'd remember Lise!

Van. Was there a Lise?
   I think she was my dream of you and me
   and how you left the mountain barren once
   when you were gone. She was my dream of you
   and how you left the Tor. Say you'll come with me.

Judith. Yes.

The Indian. It's a long day's work to dig a grave
   in stony ground. But you're young and have good
                                   shoulders.
   It should be done tonight.

Van. I'll have it done
   even if you don't need it. Tell me the place.

The Indian. There's still an Indian burying ground that
                                   lies
   behind the northern slope. Beneath it runs
   a line of square brown stones the white men used
   to mark their dead. Below still, in a ring,
   are seven graves, a woman and six men,
   the Indians killed and laid there. In the freshet,
   after the rain last night, the leaf-mould washed,
   and the seven looked uncovered at the sky,

white skeletons with flintlocks by their sides,
and on the woman's hand a heavy ring
made out of gold. I laid them in again.

Van. Seven graves—a woman and six men—
Maybe they'll rest now.

The Indian. Dig them in deeper, then.
They're covered only lightly.

Van. I'll dig them deeper.

The Indian. But you must make my grave with my own
people,
higher, beneath the ledge, and dig it straight,
and narrow. And you must place me in the fashion
used by the Indians, sitting at a game,
not fallen, not asleep. And set beside me
water and food. If this is strange to you,
think only I'm an Indian with strange ways,
but I shall need them.

Van. Don't worry. You shall have it
just the way you want it.

The Indian. Shall we go?

Van. One last look at the rock. It's not too late
to hold out on the bargain. Think of the gouge
they'll make across these hills.

Judith. If it's for me
you sell, we'll have enough without it, Van.
We'll have each other.

Van. Oh, but you were right.
When they wash over you, you either swim
or drown. We won't be here.

The Indian. And there's one comfort.
 I heard the wise Iachim, looking down
 when the railroad cut was fresh, and the bleeding earth
 offended us. There is nothing made, he said,
 and will be nothing made by these new men,
 high tower, or cut, or buildings by a lake
 that will not make good ruins.

Judith. Ruins? This?

The Indian. Why, when the race is gone, or looks aside
 only a little while, the white stone darkens,
 the wounds close, and the roofs fall, and the walls
 give way to rains. Nothing is made by men
 but makes, in the end, good ruins.

Van. Well, that's something.
 But I can hardly wait.

CURTAIN